Spiritual
DETOX

Create in me a clean heart, O God,
and renew a steadfast spirit within me.
(Psalm 51:10)

Spiritual **DETOX**

Don Egan

The RSVP Trust
PO Box 55, Stowmarket, IP14 1UG, England

ISBN   978-0-9554390-0-1

Scripture quotations, unless otherwise indicated, are from
the New King James Version.

Used with permission.

Published by
The RSVP Trust
P O Box 55, Stowmarket, Suffolk, IP14 1UG, England

Acknowledgements

Many thanks to Julia Waller for reading the manuscript and suggesting changes. To Adam Waller for his encouragement. Also to Martin Garner for your friendship and inspiration and your stories. Thanks to all the guys on the Associates Retreat - everyone of you makes an impact on me more than you know.

Thanks to J John for your encouragement and friendship and the cover quote.

Thanks to my daughter Beckie for the cover design.

And thanks to Andy Economides who told me I must write books.

Contents

Incident at Miriam Street.

When I was about ten years old, I went to the local shop to buy some chocolate. While I was paying for my purchase I heard a commotion outside the shop. A van had stopped in the road and one of its front wheels had dropped into a hole in the road so the vehicle was grounded on the road's surface. A group of men helped the driver to recover the van from the hole. As they stood back to look at the hole, I came out of the shop, with a few others, to see what was happening. We were all amazed as the hole kept growing before our eyes. Within half an hour there was a hole in the road the size of a house. It transpired that the old Victorian sewer had collapsed.

For years following that incident, roads all over Manchester collapsed as the old sewers gave way. The Victorians had built the impressive sewer system but no one had really bothered to maintain it. Without the care needed, the sewers finally disintegrated all over the city. That which was unseen, beneath the surface, had been neglected. Eventually, the inevitable collapse came.

From time to time the same thing happens to human beings. We are astonished when leaders fall from grace. It surprises us when Church leaders fall or lose their faith. If we neglect what's happening beneath the surface of our life, collapse will come as surely as an untended garden is overrun by weeds.

There are plenty of people who appear to be religious and moral. Every Sunday they put on their church face and go to church smiling and acting like everything's fine. Having a good outward appearance is easy to achieve. Living the reality is much harder. What really matters is what is in our heart, our spirit.

> "For what man knows the things of a man except the spirit of the man which is in him?"
>
> (1 Cor 2:11)

My purpose, in this book, is to help you detox your inner life. Detox is the modern abbreviation of the word 'detoxify', meaning to purge something of toxins or poisons. God is a holy God and he does not share his glory with another. He is pure. In John 10:10, Jesus tells us Satan's purpose for your life and then goes on to tell us of His purpose for your life.

> "The thief does not come except to steal, and to kill, and to destroy. I have come that they may have life, and that they may have it more abundantly."

'*Steal*', '*kill*' and '*destroy*' are the hallmarks of Satan. I have had the sadness of knowing several church leaders who experienced 'inner collapse'. Two committed suicide. One was imprisoned for fraud. Another was exposed as a paedophile. Others committed adultery or were eliminated by the enemy some other way. Some just lost their faith or became exhausted and gave up. The common denominator in all these cases is that Satan eliminated all of them through his plan to steal, kill and destroy.

As I write this, I have just heard of another leader, with huge potential, who has left his wife and is on the run from the police who want to question him about allegations of fraud. I hope the story proves false but it will not surprise me if it is true.

Please understand that there is nothing written in this book that is intended to condemn anyone. I will touch on sensitive issues but my purpose is to help you find true freedom to be yourself. I have tried, where appropriate, to share my own walk out of darkness to illustrate that it is possible to be free. I also know that I still have battles to fight - it's a lifelong process and the enemy is unrelenting.

Saint Paul, who wrote most of the New Testament, wrestled with these inner conflicts. He frankly spelled out his inner conflict and admitted that he often failed to do what he knew was right.

His honesty gives gives us hope.

"I do not understand what I do. For what I want to do, I do not do, but what I hate, I do. And if I do what I do not want to do, I agree that the law is good. As it is, it is no longer I myself who do it, but it is sin living in me. I know that nothing good lives in me, that is, in my sinful nature. For I have the desire to do what is good, but I cannot carry it out. For what I do, is not the good I want to do; no, the evil I do not want to do - this I keep on doing. Now if I do what I do not want to do, it is no longer I who do it, but it is sin living in me that does it. So I find this law at work: When I want to do good, evil is right there with me. For in my inner being I delight in God's law; but I see another law at work in the members of my body, waging war against the law of my mind and making me a prisoner of the law of sin at work within my members. What a wretched man I am! Who will rescue me from this body of death? Thanks be to God - through Jesus Christ our Lord!"
(Romans 7:15-25, NIV)

I know for a fact that if a special group of men had not invested time in me and had not imparted some integrity to me, I would have fallen a long time ago. This 'inner collapse' would have happened to me.

By contrast, Jesus' plan for your life is abundance. Abundance means 'more than enough'. It's a concept foreign to many people. Some time ago, my little grandson, Tyler, asked if he could pour his own drink. I agreed. I put a glass on the worktop and he began to pour the drink. It reached the top of the glass but he just kept pouring. I told him to stop but he just kept pouring. It went all over the worktop down the cupboards and all over the kitchen floor. He just kept pouring and his smile turned to laughter. My mindset was 'enough will do'. His mindset was 'abundance' - more than enough. What Tyler did is much closer to Jesus' plan for your life than what I would have done. That's why Jesus said we must come as little children, if we are to enter the kingdom of heaven.

He wants you to have more than enough. His only condition is that he is your only source of supply and that you don't pollute your relationship with him with spiritual toxins from other sources.

Some of the things in this book are probably not affecting you right now. Others most certainly are. My hope is that, together, we can identify anything that is spiritually toxic and eliminate it from your life.

Jesus himself told people who were established in spiritual matters, that just having the appearance of spirituality is not enough. To appear holy and spiritual on the outside and neglect what is going on inside us, is death.

"Woe to you, scribes and Pharisees, hypocrites! For you cleanse the outside of the cup and dish, but *inside* they are full of extortion and self-indulgence. Blind Pharisee, first *cleanse the inside* of the cup and dish, that the outside of them may be clean also. Woe to you, scribes and Pharisees, hypocrites! For you are like whitewashed tombs which indeed appear beautiful outwardly, but *inside* are full of dead men's bones and all uncleanness. Even so you also outwardly appear righteous to men, but *inside* you are full of hypocrisy and lawlessness."
(Matthew 23: 25-28)

Jesus came to make us clean on the inside. His primary tool for cleansing us is his word. He tells us that he continues to prune or 'cleanse' us so that we can be more fruitful.

"Every branch in Me that does not bear fruit He takes away; and every branch that bears fruit He prunes, that it may bear more fruit. You are already *clean because of the*

word which I have spoken to you."
(John 15:2)

The early disciples continued in this teaching of 'detoxing' or cleansing their lives.

"Therefore, having these promises, beloved, let us cleanse ourselves from all filthiness of the flesh and spirit, perfecting holiness in the fear of God."
(2 Cor 7:1)

I want to look at seven areas of our life, that we should detox, under the following headings:

1. Detox your past
2. Detox your thoughts
3. Detox your words
4. Detox your actions
5. Detox your habits
6. Detox your character
7. Detox your destiny

The key to success.
Your thoughts create your words. Your words create your actions. Your actions create your habits. Your habits create your character. Your character creates your destiny. So your thoughts effectively create your destiny. And, for most of us, our thoughts are greatly influenced by our past. But they don't need to be.

1. Detox your past

My friend Martin Garner was asked to speak at a conference. As an introduction to his talk, he told the audience about '*daddy-daughter-time*'. His daughters, aged eleven and twelve, have an hour each, every week, where they have his complete attention. They can do anything they want and normally go for a hot chocolate or a burger meal somewhere. The hour is spent talking about life, boys, money, fears, hopes, dreams and anything that is important to the girls. Martin uses these times to build up and affirm his daughters on a one to one basis. As he shared this simple story about relationships with his daughters, several women burst into tears and some walked out of the room. Fortunately, some people were on hand to pray with these ladies. Each one shared a sad story of neglect, hurt or loss in connection with their father. Martin's story of a loving relationship with his daughters had stirred deep emotional feelings in these women. Feelings that had lain unresolved for decades. Unresolved issues in our past can poison the present and rob us of our future.

Life is not fair. But I'm not entirely sure why we think it should be. When God placed men and women in the garden of Eden, he gave instructions about how the world worked and how to live blessed lives in peace. Since the day men and women rejected God's way and chose their own way, life has not been fair. The long shadow of man's immaturity and sinfulness falls across the whole earth. Life is not fair. Bad stuff happens to good people. Jesus told us to expect trouble in this life.

> "I have told you these things, so that in me you may have peace. In this world you will have trouble. But take heart! I have overcome the world."
>
> (John 16:33 NIV)

It's not really what happens to us in life that matters but how we respond to what happens. Nelson Mandela was imprisoned by the racist South African authorities and abused for the best part of three decades. But this man, largely due to what was inside him, went from prisoner to President - in one leap. He did not allow himself to become poisoned by hatred, even though he was abused horrifically and would have been justified in doing so. He detoxed his past. In his autobiography 'Long Walk to Freedom', he writes,

> "It was during those long and lonely years that my hunger for the freedom of my own people became a hunger for the freedom of all people, white and black. I knew as well as anything that the oppressor must be liberated just as surely as the

oppressed. A man who takes away another man's freedom is a prisoner of hatred, he is locked behind the bars of prejudice and narrow-mindedness. I am not truly free if I am taking away someone else's freedom, just as I am not free when my freedom is taken from me. The oppressed and the oppressor alike are robbed of their humanity."

As an old man, who suffered abuse and wrongful imprisonment for most of his life for the crime of being black, Nelson Mandela exudes an unexpected peace and inner joy. He seems totally free of hurt and bitterness. His smile lights up the room whenever he appears. It's his most noticeable feature. He has let go of his past and forgiven his enemies. These are two keys to detoxing our past.

Saint Paul was another man beaten and abused for the crime of becoming a Christian. He applied the same principle.

"...one thing I do: Forgetting what is behind and straining towards what is ahead, I press on towards the goal to win the prize for which God has called me heavenwards in Christ Jesus."
(Philipians 3:13-14, NIV)

It's not easy to let go of our past but it is possible and it is necessary. One of the most impressive speakers I have ever heard is the American Bible teacher Joyce Meyer. Joyce was sexually abused by her father as a child and, as a result, grew up with very low self esteem. This made it very difficult for her to have stable relationships, particularly with men. Yet today, it would be hard to imagine anyone more free from their past and present trials.

Suffering sexual abuse as a child and enduring a failed first marriage, Joyce discovered the freedom to live victoriously by applying God's Word to her life and in turn desires to help others do the same. From her battle with breast cancer to the struggles of everyday life, she speaks openly and practically about her experiences so others can apply what she has learned to their lives.

Over the years, God has provided Joyce with many opportunities to share her testimony and the life-changing message of the Gospel. Recently, Time magazine selected her as one of the most influential evangelical leaders in America. She is an incredible testimony of the dynamic and redeeming work of Jesus Christ. She believes and teaches that, regardless of a person's background or past mistakes, God has a place for them and can help them on their path to enjoying everyday life. Her life is proof that God can heal you everywhere you hurt.

I think one of the greatest statements in the Bible is made by Saint Paul when he says, "None of these things move me." He says this at the end of a list of his past difficulties and expected future difficulties.

"And see, now I go bound in the spirit to Jerusalem, not knowing the things that will happen to me there, except that the Holy Spirit testifies in every city, saying that chains and tribulations await me. But none of these things move me."
(Acts 20:22-24)

Bad things are almost certain to happen to you sometime or another. The question is, will you allow those things to 'move you'? In other words, will those things be your driving force? Admiral Nelson suffered seasickness for most of his life but he chose not to let it move him - not to let it rob him of his destiny. Many people have allowed their past to rob them of their destiny.

When I was a teenager, I was beaten up almost every day at high school. Sometimes it happened in front of the teachers and they did nothing about it. When I left school and got a job, I was exploited by several employers, working long hours for very little pay and in conditions that would not be allowed today. When our son was born he had a heart deformity and was a sick child for most of his life. When he was almost three years old, he needed a second heart operation. It wasn't successful and he died in the operating theatre. About the same time my mother suddenly died from liver failure. Then, shortly after, my father died of cancer. We also messed up our finances and fell into crippling debt, which took us years to pay off. Life is not fair. But you know what? I can say with Saint Paul, 'None of these things move me'. Those things are not the driving force of my life. Those who hurt me, I have forgiven. I do not intend allowing them to hurt me again but nor do I hold any bitterness against them.

Many people complain that they didn't have certain things when they were young. They use this as the reason why they can't do certain things today. Listen. No one had everything when they were little but everybody had something. There is no future in your past and you need to let it go. You need to say with Paul, "...one thing I do: Forgetting what is behind and straining towards what is ahead, I press on towards the goal to win the prize for which God has called me".

Forgiveness.

In order to detox your past, you will have to let certain things go. It's very probable you will have to forgive someone who has hurt you. "But you don't understand!" you say. "You don't realise what I suffered!" Listen, I am not saying you should let someone abuse you again but you can let go of your hatred of them.

Hatred and unforgiveness fester and grow. We talk about 'nursing a grudge'. If we nurse a baby grudge, it will grow and develop into an adult grudge and eventually consume us completely.

I know forgiveness is not always easy. We all know that. But it is necessary if we are to get rid of the toxin unforgiveness produces.

When I was in training I spent two months working with the chaplains at Wansdworth Prison. All human life was there - from an architect who had embezzled money from a company, to petty criminals and murderers. One day I visited the cell of a convicted paedophile. It was not his first sentence. He was obsessed with nine year old boys. All his victims were nine year old boys. He had been in various treatment programmes but nothing had worked. As we talked, he confided in me that his own father had sexually assaulted him when he was nine years old. I didn't need to be a therapist to see that this man was trapped in the situation with his father and was reliving the experience by sexually assaulting boys who were the same age as he had been when the assault took place.

I asked him if he had ever thought of forgiving his father. He was shocked and laughed nervously. "Well, I've been through all the treatments on offer" he said, "but no one has ever suggested that!" I tried to show him that by releasing his father he would also begin to release himself. We talked about the idea a little more. He was an intelligent man and saw how it would work but then said "No. I will never forgive him for what he did to me." And so he remained trapped. His story is the exact opposite of Joyce Meyer's story. Joyce is able to visit her father and have a proper relationship with him now. I doubt the man in Wandsworth Prison ever will.

The first step in forgiving someone who has hurt us is to be willing to forgive. You may not feel, at the outset, that you can forgive. But are you *willing* to let Jesus make you willing? It is something that Jesus does inside you, in the secret place. Are you willing to let Jesus make you willing to forgive? You could close your eyes and picture the person who has hurt you standing with Jesus. "Lord," you could pray,"you know how they have hurt me, but today I am willing for you to make me willing to forgive them". Let Jesus in.

In certain parts of Africa they catch monkeys.
They tie a small jar, with a narrow neck, to the ground. In the jar they place a nut as bait for the monkey. Along comes the monkey and sees the jar and looks in and sees the nut he wants. He puts his hand into the jar - his empty hand will just fit through the neck of the jar. He grabs the nut and then discovers that he can't get his hand out and he is trapped. Actually, he is free to go at any time. All he has to do is let go of the nut and his empty hand will come out of the jar. But he will not let go of the nut. He just won't. So the men who set the trap come and kill the monkey. Satan does the same thing to people but he uses past hurts instead of nuts. When we refuse to let go of the past and unforgiveness, his plan to steal, kill and destroy is complete.

Forgiveness is a mechanism of freedom - it's a complete package. Live in forgiveness and you will experience forgiveness. Don't and you won't.

> "For if you forgive men when they sin against you, your heavenly Father will also forgive you. But if you do not forgive men their sins, your Father will not forgive your sins."
> (Matthew 6:14-15)

There are three very unfortunate consequences of unforgiveness. Firstly, you will find no solutions. While you are harbouring hatred and unforgiveness, it is not possible to to resolve a situation satisfactorily.

Secondly, you will live in constant conflict. People who won't forgive live with a trail of conflicts in their relationships.

Thirdly, the past will still rule you. It is virtually imposible to press on positively into your future while living in unforgiveness because the unresolved relationships still have control over your life.

The truth is, other people will hurt you at some future point in your life. You do not have the capacity or ability to hold the whole world in unforgiveness. It will destroy you in the end. It is toxic. Let it go now and step into true freedom.

A Prayer

Lord Jesus,
You know how much I have been hurt in my past. You know how it is poisoning my life. But it is so hard to forgive and let those things go. Today I ask you to come into my life, into my heart, and change me.
Make me willing to forgive those who have hurt me. I put the whole situation into your hands. Please come and set me free.
Amen

Please help me to trust men, and particularly in relationships

Desperate Housewives

When I am in East Africa, I am always amazed at how many children can speak a little English. Most uneducated children can say two English phrases. When they see my white face they run up to me and say "How are you?" When I reply and ask them the same question they say, "I am fine." That's usually where the conversation ends because that's all the English they know and I don't know any of their language. It's not real communication. It's just a phrase and quite unsatisfying for both parties.

These children remind me of so many adults in the UK who cannot speak about their feelings. When you ask them how they are, all they can say is, "I'm fine." They cannot communicate their feelings, so they just say, 'I'm fine.'

One of my favourite TV series was '*Desperate Housewives*'. There, in Wisteria Lane, all the lawns are manicured. The houses are photogenic. And everyone smiles and says, "I'm fine" when asked how they are. But the series began with a suicide behind one of the neatly painted front doors. And each week the viewer discovered yet another dark secret, behind another perfect front door in Wisteria Lane. I think it was one of the best commentaries on modern life in the Western world.

Each one of us lives in Wisteria Lane. The

lawns are kept manicured and the doors nicely painted. The white picket fence denotes our border with the outside world. But behind each door there is a dark secret that no one else in the street knows. And we desperately spend our lives managing this secret so we don't ever have to talk about our feelings. It's so exhausting.

It's hard to express our feelings because we are not sure what the listener may do with the disclosures. They may get the wrong idea and spread false rumours about us. That's why true communication can be quite alarming for so many people. Yet just walking through our day saying, repeatedly, 'How are you?' and 'I am fine', is very unsatisfying for human beings.

So feelings aren't really talked about. They're talked around. If people feel strongly about something, they'll argue about it but often, everyone talks at once and no one gets listened too. If we can't express our feelings because of feeling dominated by others or through our own timidity, we have to store them somewhere.

We've all read harrowing newspaper stories of serial murderers like Fred West, who murdered people and then had to hide the bodies. His neighbours thought he was a bit odd but they had no idea of all the bodies buried on his property. When the tragedy was uncovered it shocked the world.

Most of us, thankfully, are not keeping dead bodies buried on our property but we do bury our feelings. Eventually we run out of space for all these unresolved feelings. Then sometimes we feel moody or strange or angry and we don't know why. It is because of all these unresolved feelings from the past that catch up with us - the rotting corpses of past hurts and disappointments.

All human beings have a bottom line reaction to things which threaten them. They make decisions based on fear or aggression. It's seen in animals too. It's sometimes called '*Fight or Flight*'. Simply put, we either run away from things or fight the threat. Aggression is really a manifestation of fear but with a decision that the threat must be eliminated. So fear is one of our deepest emotions. F.E.A.R. stands for **F**alse **E**vidence **A**ppearing **R**eal. Studies have shown that over 90% of what people worry about never happens. So we can waste a lot of time running away from things that never happen.

A friend of mine ran away from a violent home when she was a teenager. She went abroad and became a model and eventually ended up addicted to drugs. She felt she was always running away. Then one day she discovered that what she was actually running away from was herself. And it doesn't matter where you go in the world, you cannot run away from yourself. Some of you reading this book have spent a lifetime on the run but you've been trying to run away from yourself. Don't you think it's time to stop this exhausting stupidity?

I have spent my life being a rather anxious man. Much of what I do causes deep feelings of fear in me. The only difference between me and many others is that I've discovered you can do things afraid. Just because you fear something doesn't mean you can't do it. You can do it afraid. You can face the fear and do it anyway.

My friend Alison visits prostitutes on the streets to introduce them to Jesus. It's a dark world I know little about. Two days ago, she asked me to go with her. It's a dark harrowing place and I was afraid. As we drove to the area, I was hoping something would happen so we didn't have to go. When we got there, I was hoping none of the ladies were out on the streets, so we could just go for coffee and talk about it instead of actually doing it. You know what? They were on the streets, we did go and I was afraid but it was alright. I have lived to tell the tale. Fear may come but it must not overcome.

The way to escape negative feelings about the past is not to run away but to do something about them. You are a valid human being. You have a right to feel angry or disappointed. You have a right to change your mind. You have a right to disagree with a group or an individual. You have a right to be yourself. It's OK to make mistakes. Your problem could just be that you have never honestly expressed yourself. Feelings shouldn't rule our lives but nor should we bury them and not express them. Sometimes we just need to be who we are, say what we really think - without qualification - and let people feel the weight of that.

Here's an exercise that may help you identify your feelings. Look at the list of feelings opposite. Over the next few days, try to think about identifying how you are feeling and start to get more aware of these feelings and how they affect you. If you identify a lot of anger, then try to look behind that anger - that will really help you deal with it more effectively.

Also look at the list of defences and do the same. Be honest with yourself and see how you act - see how you feel. Remember that feelings don't have to be negative - if they are, there is a way out and that way is by doing something about them.

Feelings

Abandoned	Adventurous	Afraid	Alone
Ambivalent	Angry	Anxious	Apathetic
Ashamed	Bewildered	Bored	Calm
Caring	Cheated	Cold	Concerned
Confident	Cowardly	Defeated	Defensive
Defiant	Discouraged	Down	Eager
Elated	Embarrassed	Energised	Envious
Excited	Failed	Fearful	Foolish
Frustrated	Grateful	Guilty	Happy
Helpless	Hesitant	Hopeless	Hostile
Hurt	Impatient	Inferior	Irrational
Jealous	Joyful	Kind	Lonely
Loving	Miserable	Natural	Nervous
Numb	Overcome	Overjoyed	Pained
Peaceful	Pious	Playful	Pleased
Proud	Provoked	Put out	Refreshed
Rejected	Reluctant	Remorseful	Resentful
Respectful	Secure	Selfish	Self-Pitying
Snappy	Stubborn	Successful	Superior
Suspicious	Tired	Tranquil	Trapped
Understood	Unhappy	Unsure	Unworthy
Used	Warm	Weary	Worthy

Defences

Agreeing	Complying	Conforming
Disagreeing	Generalising	'I don't know'
Justifying	Levity	Living 'In your head'
Making excuses	Shifting	Silence
Verbosity	'Yes, but....'	

2. Detox your thoughts

Your thoughts are incredibly powerful. What you spend your time thinking about will determine what you do in life. How you see yourself in your thoughts will determine your actions. The Bible says, "For as he thinks in his heart, so is he." (Proverbs 23:7) In other words, the way a person thinks about themself, is the way they will act. Your thoughts are really the engine of your life. What you give your attention to, will give birth to certain things in your life. I want to look in this section at several ways we need to detox our thought life.

Don't let your thoughts snowball downhill

Have you ever noticed how uptight you feel when your thoughts spiral out of control? And the more you get involved in what's troubling you, the worse you feel. One thought leads to another, then another, then another until you feel really agitated.

You know how it is. You're just going to sleep and you suddenly remember something you have to do tomorrow. You turn over to go to sleep but you start thinking about all the other things you have to do tomorrow. Then you remember a situation that's been going on for weeks that hasn't been resolved. You begin rehearsing different scenarios in your head about what you could do to change things. Then you start thinking about how stressful your life is right now. Then you remember something your spouse said earlier in the day. What did they mean? You open your eyes and there they are, lying next to you sleeping soundly. You lay on your back and stare at the ceiling and you begin to wonder if anyone on planet earth really appreciates you at all! On and on it goes until you are completely wound up. Some people do this day after day, for hours at a time and it gets them nowhere.

You need to learn to nip that sort of thinking in the bud and take control of your thoughts.

A practice I have used for many years, when the snowball thinking starts, is to stop and imagine Jesus in the room with me right now. He is the Prince of Peace, so there's no way he would come with me into snowball thinking. Then I try to listen to him. I say to him, under my breath, 'Lord, what are you saying to me right now? Anytime the snowball tries to get my attention back, I try to imagine Jesus' face. Is he smiling? Is he sad? What is he thinking? This always distracts me from the pointless snowball thinking and so peace comes. Sometimes it's easier than other times but it does work.

Then, sometimes I think, the day I die, my 'in tray' will still be full. When they put me in the ground the world will not stop. I am not the centre of the universe and, with respect, neither are you. Charles de Gaulle said, "The graveyards are full of indispensable men."

If you suffer from a lot of snowball thinking you may need to go for a long walk. My friend Martin Garner says, **'Solitude brings perspective'.** Sometimes, if we are getting stressed, we need to step away from the situation. Close up, we can't see the wood for the trees. But when we step away for a while, and find a little solitude, perspective comes.

Leonardo da Vinci once wrote: "Every now and then go away, have a little relaxation, for when you come back to your work your judgement will be surer; since to remain constantly at work will cause you to lose power of judgement. Go some distance away because the work appears smaller and more of it can be taken in at a glance, and a lack of harmony or proportion is more readily seen."

When the tide comes in, it doesn't rush in all in one movement. The waves come in and then fall back. It's a rhythmic movement of gradual advance. I think being by the sea is relaxing because we hear the rhythm of life in the sea. In the life of Jesus we see the same rhythm.

He took the disciples aside to teach them. Then he sends them out. Then he calls them aside again. Then he sends them out again. Then he calls them back to himself. Then he sends them out. Can't you almost hear the waves of his peace lapping across the pages of the Bible? So we must find this rhythm, this peace, in Him.

Deal with your anger

A person is just about as big as the things that make them angry. Everywhere I go in Britain today, people seem angry. I recently stopped at some traffic lights. There was one car in front of me. When the lights turned green, he didn't move. I waited a moment, to give him time. When it became apparent that he hadn't seen the green light. I gently sounded my horn. Immediately he began speaking in 'sign language' to me. On another occasion, a man drove on the wrong side of the road straight at me. When he had to slow down to get past me, he wound down his window and called me a "******* moron spastic!" I'm not sure what one of those is but I don't think it was a complement.

When the girls were little, I was in the kitchen trying to make some coffee. I was in the middle of a difficult situation and feeling quite insecure. The girls were making a noise and being awkward, repeatedly asking for something and wouldn't back down. I kept telling them to be quiet and go play outside for a while. On and on it went. I became very stressed. Then I snapped. I slammed the cup down on the worktop so hard the handle came off. I yelled at the top of my voice at the girls. I could feel the veins in my head sticking out. It was one of the best shouting fits I've ever had. Needless to say, the girls were crying and the atmosphere was unpleasant for sometime afterwards. I was shaking.

Later that day, I tried running upstairs to get something. As I did, an intense pain shot through the back of my head. It was so painful, it brought me to my knees. It took about two hours to fully subside. For the rest of the week it kept happening. If I dug the garden, ran down the street, or tried to lift something heavy, this terrible pain would come and cripple me. I went to the doctor and he did some tests. He couldn't find what was wrong but gave me some very strong painkillers. Next time it happened I took the pain killers. But they were so strong they put me to sleep for half a day.

I began to pray and ask God what was happening. Straight away, I felt God say, "You gave way to anger and gave the devil a foothold. When you repent of your anger the pain will go".

I wasn't expecting that. I repented of the

anger and said sorry to the girls and asked their forgiveness. When I put everything right, the pain never came back. I learnt a lesson that day. **Letting our anger rule our life, even for a brief moment, can poison our body, our mind and our spirit.**

We all feel angry from time to time and there's nothing wrong with that. God doesn't tell us not to *feel* angry.

"Be angry, and do not sin : do not let the sun go down on your wrath, nor give place to the devil."
(Eph 4: 26-27)

There's nothing wrong in *feeling* angry, it's how we process that anger that really counts. The Bible tells us not to give the devil a 'foothold'.

When I go climbing with my friend Adam, he always tries to get me to push myself a bit further and try climbing something a bit more difficult than I would normally try. He stands on the ground holding my safety rope. When I get stuck he shouts to me to tell me where the next foothold is. If I can get that foothold I can progress up the climb. If I can't get the foothold, I fall off and Adam lowers me down on the rope.

The devil is looking for footholds to make progress into your life to steal, kill and destroy. If you don't give him any he will fall off your life.

On 30th June 2003, the papers carried a story of a man who shot his neighbour over a dispute about the front hedge. Neighbours say the two men had argued over the hedge and a tree separating their front lawns. The argument reached a climax when one of the men allegedly stepped over the border and levelled a gun at his neighbour. He shot him four times from just a few feet away - even shooting him as he lay on the ground - then went back home and shut himself inside. He was arrested at the end of a three-hour siege.

> Jesus said, "You have heard that it was said to those of old, 'You shall not murder, and whoever murders will be in danger of the judgement.' But I say to you that whoever is angry with his brother without a cause shall be in danger of the judgement."
> (Matthew 5:21-22)

I find that people who are constantly angry have a root of insecurity in their life. The word '*anger*' is one letter removed from '*danger*' If you fly into a rage, you can be sure of a bad landing. When our emotions are out of control, so is our life. Anger makes our mouth work faster than our mind. We end up saying and doing things we will regret later.

Anger is like a theatre curtain ready to part for the first act of the play. Behind the curtain stand all our lonely feelings - the actors ready to perform. Guilt projection, discontentment, discouragement, abandonment, despair, unending feelings of inadequacy. Anger is the curtain that hides all these feeling from the outside world.

It's easier to be angry than to deal with the real feelings - then people won't see how much you're really hurting because anger keeps people away.

The Bibles says, "A soft answer turns away wrath, but a harsh word stirs up anger." (Proverbs 15:1) This tells us that we have a choice about being angry and that we can even affect the anger of others by giving a soft or gentle answer and keeping our cool. Getting into a rage doesn't make us 'big' or clever. In fact, the opposite is true.

> "He who is slow to anger is better than the mighty, And he who rules his spirit than he who takes a city."
>
> (Proverbs 16:32)

The Bible says, 'Do not let the sun go down on your anger'. We must deal with our anger the day we feel it. To let anger run on and on is a sin. And sin leads to death. Unresolved anger is a toxin that will destroy us if we let it build up inside of us. We do have a choice to deal with our deeper feelings and issues or to be angry and keep people away. But when we let anger rule us we disobey God and allow the devil control over our life.

Sometimes our anger is rooted in the fact that we don't like ourselves. I mean, we're just not happy living with ourselves and so we don't want anyone else to get too close. They may want us to talk about things that we haven't yet dealt with ourselves.

God likes you. He likes you so much, he says he loves you. He likes you just as you are but he likes you too much to let you stay as you are. He loves you so much, he let his Son die in your place. If you were the only person on planet earth he needed to do that for, he would have still come and died for you. Now that is true love. So, if God thinks you're so great, what is your problem?

If you feel angry a lot of the time, go back over the list of feelings in the previous section and write down any that you recognise as applying to you. Ask God to show you the root of these feelings. Then ask him to heal any hurts you may be carrying and ask him if there is anything you should do about them. God can heal you everywhere you hurt.

When we get hurt and angry we want someone to blame. We want justice. But we need to

<u>remember that God is the judge.</u> He will make everything right that is wrong. The Bible says,

> "Be still before the LORD and wait patiently for him; *do not fret* when men succeed in their ways, when they carry out their wicked schemes. *Refrain from anger* and *turn from wrath*; do not fret - it leads only to evil. For evil men will be cut off, but those who hope in the LORD will inherit the land. A little while, and the wicked will be no more; though you look for them, they will not be found. But the meek will inherit the land and enjoy great peace."
>
> (Psalm 37:7-11)

I have a sneaking suspicion that God gets justice for me when I obey him. In my life, I have found that people who attack me without cause, seem to get judgement visited on them. The most striking incident was when I was a child. A boy humiliated me because I came from a poor home. He lived on the new estate in a brand new house with his rich parents. His taunts hurt me at the time. His attack was without cause. About five years later, his house fell down. I mean, it just fell down! And there seemed to be a problem with the insurance and it was never rebuilt. Now who looked poor? These things may just be coincidence, but I've noticed it many times in my life. It never happens, though, when I try and get my own justice.

Those trying to justify anger, talk about 'righteous anger' and quote the story of Jesus making a whip and turning over the tables in the temple. There is such a thing as righteous anger, but I never met anyone who talked about it who wasn't just trying to justify their unrighteous anger and avoid dealing with the deeper insecurities they had. So I don't buy that argument most of the time.

Unresolved anger is poison and we need to keep it out of our lives by dealing with it at the time it happens. Not storing it all up so it explodes onto our innocent family or friends. If we fail to deal with our anger, our anger will deal with us. We also need to spend our time thinking good thoughts, not constantly brooding over hurts or rejection. We can choose what we think about. We can't stop birds landing on our head but we can stop them making a nest in our hair.

A prayer
Lord Jesus,
You are the Prince of peace.
You are my healer.
Please come and take away all my hurts.
Wash me clean of unforgiveness, bitterness and anger.

Prince of peace, come and live in my heart.
Let your living waters wash my soul of the
poison of unresolved anger.
Today I declare that goodness and mercy will
follow me all the days of my life.
I forgive all those who have hurt me in the
past.
Father, forgive me for all those I have hurt.
From this day, I want to walk in your peace.
Amen

Avoid pornography

A bishop was praying, at a conference, for people to be delivered from things that were holding them back. A well spoken man in his late fifties came for prayer. He leaned close to the Bishop's ear and whispered. It was difficult to hear but the Bishop thought he heard the man say, "I can't stop watching the news." A little puzzled, the Bishop replied, "The news? I don't think that's a sin. I quite like to watch the lunch time news myself, most days."

"No. No." whispered the man. "The nudes. I can't stop watching the nudes!"

This story is amusing but being a captive to pornography is not. Pornography is a spirit and it will poison your thoughts. When I was twelve years old, my friends and I met some other boys who told us that someone had dumped a large amount of 'dirty magazines' in the park. The news spread quickly and we set off in search of what we thought was 'treasure'. Back then, in the 1960's, pictures of naked women were something teenage boys heard about and talked about, but actually seeing one was very rare, certainly in my sheltered life. We arrived at the scene and, sure enough, there was a huge pile of magazines full of topless and naked women. Today, you will probably see more female flesh next to the Radio Times in Asda or on page three of The Sun, but back then it was very rare for young boys to have access to such images. Today, you are only ever 'two clicks' away from pornography on the internet.

My story could sound like a few boys having a bit of naughty fun and no harm was done. But in reality, harm was done. We spent hours in the park that day ogling the pictures, filling our heads with inappropriate images of women. It was hard to break away from it and that's my point - pornography is very addictive.

Looking at those pictures of anonymous women was the worst possible introduction a young boy could have to sexual relationships. It introduces the idea that women are objects to be used and abused. From that day on, I discovered that pornography has a voice. It calls to the ones it captivates and it calls to children. I was surprised how many times I would find a discarded magazine when I was walking somewhere alone and I was always powerless - I had to kick open the pages and look. Eventually, it got to the point where I couldn't think straight about anything without my mind sexualising it. I went to see a couple of ladies who had a healing ministry at church. It was very embarrassing but I told them the whole sorry tale. As they prayed for me they laid hands on my head and asked Jesus to cleanse my mind. As they did this an immense burning sensation passed through my brain. It was so searing I thought my hair would burst into flames. From that hour, I could not remember even one of the images I had seen. I was totally set free.

Today sexual images come at us from every direction, in every shop, magazine, TV channel and, of course, the internet. Children younger than I was, are being exposed to far more extreme images and there will be consequences - for the individual, for women and for society.

That day in the park, we thought we had found a massive amount of images of topless ladies. But today our nation is being hit by a *'pornography tsunami'*.

It is safe to assume that most men and most women have seen pornography on the internet at some time.

In 1998, there were 28,000 'adult' sites on the internet making £1.5 billion a year. Three years later, in 2001, the number of sites had increased to 280,000 and made profits of £15- £30 billion. Over one million internet sites are now 'X rated' It is now truer to say 'there's a little internet on the pornography' rather than 'there's pornography on the internet'.

Some statistics

Recent studies showed:

80% of Internet traffic is pornography related.
50% of teens say they have seen pornography on the Internet.
79% of these teens did so from their school or public library.
67% of these same teens did so from home.
12 is the average age of a child's first experience with pornography.

A businessman worked in an office down the corridor from his two colleagues. He began using e-mail and SMS messages to communicate with them instead of walking down the corridor and speaking to them face to face. Eventually, all his communication was electronic and he never met his colleagues in person. He lost his real relationship with them and only encountered them 'electronically'.

Pornography works the same way. It begins to replace real relationships with a digital encounter. We end up with pornography instead of an intimate marriage relationship. What really satisfies us is relationships - that's what we were designed for. Pornography always leads to increasing isolation. It isolates us and causes men, in particular, to live in an imagined world attended by what C S Lewis called, 'a harem of fantasy brides'. Lewis was not unfamiliar with his dark side. He looked inside himself and was appalled by what he saw - as he put it, "A Zoo of lusts, a bedlam of ambitions, a nursery of fears, a harem of fondled hatreds."

We *can* choose what images we put into our eyes. Some people love to watch surgical operations on TV. Personally, I don't. I choose to go out of the room if that's on. We have choices. *You* have choices.

The Bible tells the stories of two leaders troubled by sexual images. One stood firm, one fell flat. Joseph resisted the seductive advances of his master's wife. David gave in to temptation and had an adulterous affair with Bathsheba. Both men had human limitations but Joseph recognised his weaknesses while David overestimated his strengths.

We need to set boundaries before temptation arises. When the alarm bells go off, we need to respond to the alarm. We need to choose to resist temptation and guard our heart in this unguarded world, because a drifting heart has only one way to go - away from God.

Sex is great. I think it's one of the best ideas God ever had. I think women are great. I think good looking women are great. I'm glad God made them. But God has set boundaries for sex.

The boundaries are one man with one woman, in marriage, for life. Anything else will involve emotional pain, mental torment, disappointment, addiction or all of the above.

Sure, we can't unscramble eggs and stuff happens. Many people are divorced and some of those people remarry. Anyone who's been through a divorce will tell you of the awful emotional pain involved. We can't unscramble eggs but we can make a good omelette with the life we have left. We *can* do the right thing from now on as far as it depends on us.

God has set boundaries for sex to keep us safe. When great rivers run within their banks, they are things of great beauty. When the river overflows and bursts its banks, it causes devastation and is viewed as a disaster. The same is true for sex. Within the boundaries set by God it is a beautiful thing. But when the boundaries get broken it leads to disaster.

The problem with all addictions is that they take the place of God. They want to be first in our attentions and they want to control us and take our time. They want to be our treasure.

Jesus said, "For where your treasure is, there your heart will be also. The lamp of the body is the eye. If therefore your eye is good, your whole body will be full of light.

But if your eye is bad, your whole body will be full of darkness. If therefore the light that is in you is darkness, how great is that darkness! No one can serve two masters; for either he will hate the one and love the other, or else he will be loyal to the one and despise the other."

(Matthew 6:21-24)

Here we can see the problem of pornography. First, it wants to be our treasure. If it is our treasure, our heart will follow it. It will lead us into deeper darkness. We will spend time thinking about it. It will promise us everything and give us nothing.

Second, the eye is the 'lamp' of the body. If we put the things of light into our eyes, we will be full of light. If we put the dark images of pornography into our eyes, we will be full of darkness. That's why pornography often causes depression and spiritual problems in those who are addicted.

Third, it wants to be our master. Pornography is essentially a spirit that wants to rule over us. It's a deception. It's a lie. It says that all these people are ready and willing to have sex with us, any way we want it. The reality is that the people in the images are are all broken, wounded people who have been, and are being, abused.

When my friend Alison began our ministry to women involved in prostitution, I left Alison and her team to it and just helped her think through each new step. But recently, I have become involved on the front line and met some of the women. I can tell you there is nothing glamourous or sexy in the sex trade. It is a deeply depressing, dark world of broken and abused people.

80,000 women are involved in the sex trade in the UK. On average, every year, most of these women will be raped nineteen times, kidnapped ten times, and beaten repeatedly. On the night I visited the streets with Alison and her husband, Richard, the first girl we met was Tracy. I thought Alison had made a mistake in chatting to Tracy, as she was only a teenager and dressed normally. She looked like she was waiting for a friend. But Tracy was waiting for 'customers'. She had got involved with an older man who groomed her for prostitution and who is now her pimp.

Sharon met us further down the street. She's twenty four. Her parents both died of heroin addiction and she is now addicted to drugs. Her leg had a weeping sore from an infection. She was talking about committing suicide. Further down the street two girls stood together, which is unusual, but one was 'training' the other in the sex trade. Another girl stood on a corner, her face etched with the abuse of her trade, making her look much older than she was.

Each naked person you look at on the screen or on the page is a real person, whom God loves, and is almost certainly suffering abuse or control. When we view pornography, we are perpetuating the misery of those involved. We are kneeling before the idol of Baal, the ancient god of sexual abuse.

> "The king ordered Hilkiah the high priest, the priests next in rank and the doorkeepers to remove from the temple of the LORD all the articles made for Baal and Asherah and all the starry hosts. He burned them outside Jerusalem in the fields of the Kidron Valley and took the ashes to Bethel... He also tore down the quarters of the *male shrine-prostitutes*, which were in the temple of the LORD..."
> (2 Kings 23:4,7)

In Leviticus 18, God lists a whole group of people we shouldn't see naked.

> "None of you shall approach anyone who is near of kin to him, to uncover his nakedness: I am the LORD."
> (Leviticus 18:6).

Our nakedness should only be shared with our spouse, if we have one. It's time some people put their clothes on. In the parable of the prodigal son, who wasted his wealth on prostitutes, it is interesting that part of his restoration was to have a robe put on him.

> "But the father said to his servants,
> 'Bring out the best robe and put it on him,
> and put a ring on his hand and sandals on
> his feet."

When God restores us, he clothes us.

Pornography is clearly linked to lust and masturbation. Most people discover masturbation around the time of puberty, when they are discovering their sexuality. And there is nothing wrong with that. It's when things become an addiction that there is a problem. The Bible nowhere mentions masturbation - it is not listed as a sin. So, if God didn't mention it, why have I? Because I think lust, pornography and masturbation are all part of the same thing.

Masturbation surely requires lustful thoughts. It's difficult to imagine a man maintaining an erection while thinking solely about broccoli, for example. Masturbation is not directly mentioned in the Bible because I don't think Jesus wants us getting hung up on all this, but I think he implies it may be a problem when connected to lust.

"You have heard that it was said to those of old, 'You shall not commit adultery.' But I say to you that whoever looks at a woman to lust for her has already committed adultery with her in his heart. If your right eye causes you to sin, pluck it out and cast it from you; for it is more profitable for you that one of your members perish, than for your whole body to be cast into hell. And if your right hand causes you to sin, cut it off and cast it from you; for it is more profitable for you that one of your members perish, than for your whole body to be cast into hell."
(Matthew 5: 27-30)

The clear progression Jesus talks about - lust, your eye and your hand - is no coincidence.

Steve Nicholson broadcasts a thought provoking podcast called, '*Christian Sexuality in a Sex-Crazed World*'. In one episode, he reads a statement from one woman about why she was addicted to masturbation.

"First of all I felt out of control and wanted control in my life. Fantasy coupled with masturbation were safer than being in real relationships with people. Fantasies can't hurt me like those who sexually abused me. I can control the fantasy. i.e. who to be with, how the partner will respond to me, what will happen, and when to feel aroused. As an abuse victim I could not control any of these. Eventually I realised the fantasies were not real and were not fulfilling. Of course, the progression of these erotic fantasies made me feel worse about myself. I returned to this addiction repeatedly when I didn't feel in control of my life. Over time I began surrendering my need to be in control. And I then entrusted Jesus to manage different areas of my life. One by one, I transferred management responsibilities of my finances, my career and my family, my school, my dating relationships, talents, success, future, my time, my self-protective mechanisms and my hurts, all to Jesus."

We all have a dark side but we need to understand that's what it is - *dark*. We need to control it and make sure it doesn't control us.

If you have become addicted to pornography, or if you've just been careless and thought there was no harm in it, you can be free of it's grip today. As with all addictions, you need to call out to Jesus to set you free. As you pray and keep on praying, he will bring you out of captivity, to freedom. It is God who will do it. He is far more powerful than any addiction that has you in its grip. The dream of being completely free can be a reality in your life. The people of Israel were in captivity for years. Then one day, God answered their prayers and set them free.

> "When the LORD brought back the captivity of Zion, we were like those who dream. Then our mouth was filled with laughter, and our tongue with singing. Then they said among the nations, "The LORD has done great things for them. The LORD has done great things for us, and we are glad."
> (Psalm 126: 1-3)

A prayer for freedom.
Lord Jesus,
I admit today that I have been addicted to pornography.
I want to be free.
I can't seem to stop this addiction.
Jesus, please come and rescue me and set me completely free.
Burn from my mind all memories of the inappropriate images I have seen.
Release me from this captivity.
Help me Jesus.
Transform me by the renewing of my mind.
I receive your healing now by faith.
Amen.

Renounce any involvement in Hypnotism

In 2005, a close friend of mine was visiting some friends from a church in America. A small group of about twenty people met in someone's home to pray and worship Jesus. As they did, a girl in the group, named Emma, began to weep. Nothing strange there. Often, when we draw close to God in intimate worship, his goodness and grace to us can seem overwhelming.

However, as the worship went on, Emma became more emotional and eventually seemed distressed. As most of the people there were young, my friend, being in her thirties, went over to reassure Emma that everything was alright. She laid a hand gently on Emma's shoulder. As she did, Emma reacted and began acting like a snake, writhing from side to side, her face contorted.

The Pastor joined my friend to pray with Emma. As he did, Emma reacted again and began speaking with a strange voice. Something demonic seemed to have her in its power and was very uncomfortable with the worship of Jesus. Recognising demonic influence, the Pastor began to rebuke the spirit and drive it out of Emma's writhing body. The spirit told the Pastor its name and the Pastor asked, "When did you enter her?"

The disturbing voice answered, "When she was weak. When she allowed herself to be hypnotised".

It turned out that Emma's parents had taken her to see an hypnotist when she was five years old to cure her bed-wetting. After over an hour of prayer, the spirit left Emma at the Pastor's command, in the name of Jesus.

Emma has been free ever since. Today she is a successful missionary who brings the peace of Jesus to many lives. It seems opening herself to a hypnotist had, for Emma, also opened a door to demonic influence.

Our soul is made up of the mind, the will and the emotions. It is connected to our spirit and is the very centre of our essence as a human being. When God created Adam and Eve he told them to dominate the whole of creation. Nowhere were they told to dominate each other. But when we allow someone to control and interfere with our mind, we allow them to dominate our soul.

In our culture, there is a 'let's embrace everything' mentality and anyone who dissents is considered narrow minded. Woolworth's idea of 'pick and mix' for sweets has long since infected religious thought and practice in the UK.

I want to explain why I believe hypnotism is a dangerous spiritual toxin. There is not room here to explore the subject exhaustively, though I will make a detailed case because, in researching this subject, I found little has been written, in any detail, about this subject by Christians. I also believe Emma's story gives us cause for concern.

The first recorded hypnotic performance was given at the court of Khufu in ancient Egypt over 5000 years ago. An account of this performance is recorded on papyrus and stored in a British museum.

Franz Mesmer, a scientist during the mid-1700's, began the foray into the scientific uses of hypnotism through his belief that magnets held healing powers. Many believed that his overwhelming presence influenced his patients to go into trances, in this way Mesmer was able to bring about the resurgence of hypnotism. Hence the phrase, 'I was mesmerised'.

A surgeon by the name of James Braid followed in the steps of Mesmer and Mesmerism, and he came up with the term *hypnotism* from the Greek word *hypnos*, which means sleep.

In 1889 Albert Moll wrote the book *Hypnotism* in which he insisted that it was a scientific subject to be included in the growing study of psychology. With the help of these men, the exploration of hypnotism's medical use as well as the debate of it as science or entertainment found its beginnings.

On its Hypnosis & Hypnotherapy FAQ page,

ukhypnosis.com asks the question, "Is hypnosis safe?" The reply is very similar to the reply you will get from most hypnotherapists. It says,

"Absolutely. There are no known records of anyone having been physically or mentally harmed as a direct result of hypnosis itself. It is utterly impossible for anyone to get 'stuck' in hypnosis."

Sadly, the truth is slightly more disturbing. Transcripts from debates in the House of Commons tell a very different story.

"Mr. Colin Pickthall (*Lancashire, West*): ...hypnotism has been a long-standing concern of mine since I was alerted to its dangers by one of my constituents, Mrs. Margaret Harper. Some years ago, her daughter, Sharon Tabarn, was hypnotised at a club in Leyland in Lancashire. At the end of the trance, she was told to come out of it as if she had had a 10,000 volt electric shock. Her husband took her home in a somewhat dazed state, and five hours later she died.

The coroner's inquest found that this was an accidental death. The expert witness, a Dr. Heap, declared that there was no connection between hypnosis and any physical side-effects. That is patent nonsense. The Home Office pathologist said: "It is hard not to think there was a link."

My view is that the coincidence is too great to be dismissed and that evidence from other incidents shows that the link is likely to be real.

I have had letters from all over the country giving disturbing accounts of the effects of stage hypnosis, some of which I have passed to the Minister. I shall give some examples. Mr. Cannon from Barnet in the summer of 1992 was hypnotised and as a result he has had violent headaches ever since. He describes it as having made his life hell. A Mr. Hill of Rotherham was hypnotised by one Henry James ... and is subject to violent headaches, violent uncontrollable anger and persistent panic attacks. He was hospitalised several times on anti- depressants and has a permanent sleeping disorder.

Dean Chambers from Blackpool had his arm paralysed for four weeks as a result of the condition under which he was placed under hypnosis. A young man from High Wycombe who was hypnotised by Paul McKenna, who is quite famous in this area, had to go to a psychiatric unit two days later where he was detained for six weeks and was still receiving treatment seven weeks later. While he was hypnotised he was put into regression, which is against the code of conduct, and was left unattended, which is also against the guidelines.

Mr. Nickson of Prestatyn became unable to work as a result of stage hypnotism, and was unable to hold a conversation and has attempted suicide. His case is attested by Mr. Trevelyn, the consultant psychiatrist for Clwyd. David Burill of Blackpool was hypnotised by Alan Bates and collapsed immediately after being brought round. He went crazy - his words - and had to be re-hypnotised by Bates. He suffered from violent headaches for weeks afterwards.

Ruth McLoughlin, a Glasgow university student, was hypnotised in October by Stefan Force and doctors found afterwards that her heart rate had dropped to a dangerously low level. Those are a few of the complaints that I and others have received.

Dr. Prem Meisra, who works in Glasgow, described a patient who... went into a trance again every time someone clapped, and a further patient began to suffer from a schizo-affective disorder.

This is plainly a highly dangerous business with potentially, perhaps actually, huge consequences for the national health service, as well as for the people concerned. In some instances, it may even have consequences for spectators.

Mr. Nirj Joseph Deva *(Brentford and Isleworth):* I am not an expert on stage hypnotism or any other form, but if one is willing to be hypnotised, one is acquiescing. It is a matter of personal choice. How does one strike a balance between personal choice and the adverse effects that may result?

Mr. Forsyth: I agree with my hon. Friend that personal choice is exerted when deciding to be hypnotised, but the whole point is that, once one is hypnotised, personal choice is somewhat diminished. That is the reasoning behind the legislation."

Here, in a debate about hypnotism, a few examples of those who have suffered strange mental and physical problems are given. But these may be only the tip of the iceberg.

Tracie O'Keefe, writing about the case of Sharron Tabarn, in a research paper, states,

"Sharron was put through several tasks during the stage hypnosis experience including imitating the pop singer Madonna, seeing the men in the audience with no clothes on and kissing a man in the audience. The suggestion given to her to terminate the trance experience was that when the hypnotist said "goodnight" the subjects would feel 10,000 volts of electricity through the seat of their chairs. As the hypnotist did this it seemed to onlookers that she flew off her chair. (Patricia Andrew, witness statement, 24.9.93) (McCann, 1993).

When Sharron was 11 years old, according to her parents, she had received an electric shock from a wall switch in the family home and it had thrown her across the room. Her parents reported that from that moment on Sharron had been terrified of electricity and as an adult would not even change a light bulb or a plug. Three or four weeks before her death her father nearly died of an electric shock and was signed off work with burns for five weeks (Interviews between Mr and Mrs Harper (Sharron's parents) & O'Keefe, 1996-97).

With people who suffer phobias the

exposure to a specific stimuli can bring on an adverse reaction in response to that imagined stimuli as if it had been real (Bourne 1995) (Andreas & Andreas 1989).

After the stage hypnosis show Sharron said that she was not feeling well so the group went back to her home. Complaining of a bad headache and dizziness, she went to lie down and slept on the bottom of her youngest daughter's bed, not even bothering to take off any of her clothes (McCann, 1993). Just after she went to bed, she was administered Paracetamol, something which Sharron's mother said was very rare (Interviews with Mr and Mrs Harper and O'Keefe, 1996-97)

At 7.00am in the morning her estranged husband Darren, who had stayed over in the same room, heard the children making a noise and when he investigated he found Sharron dead at the bottom of the bed (McCann, 1993).

To imply that hypnosis is benign is, in fact, incorrect because its very induction is dependent upon suggestions changing the psychological and physical qualities of the subject."

Two small children were left without a mother. The father of those children was left with the burden of bringing them up as a single parent. Her parents and sister also suffered a great loss and continue to feel cheated because they believe that her death was not sufficiently investigated.

Twenty years before, in the north of England, Sonia Cunningham, a young woman, died in similar circumstances. Her death occurred less than 24 hours after being involved in hypnosis. In that district an immediate ban on stage hypnosis was taken up by the local authority and is still in force today.

To control others by overriding their will could be seen as mental assault. If we compare it to physical assault, even if consent was given, it does not make it morally right.

Using a telephone is legal. Tapping into someone's telephone line and interfering with their affairs is not. This is effectively what hypnotism does, albeit with consent but often unwitting consent. But don't take my word for it. Let's hear from an ex-hypnotherapist. His website states,

> "In the late 1980's Dr. Jeremy Wheeler trained as a hypnotherapist, and later diverted into stage hypnosis. Most of his hypnotic shows emanated from re-bookings making him one of the busiest comedy hypnotists in the business. Giving

up a profession that was earning him a small fortune, for very little work, was hard to walk away from. Jeremy feels it is only morally right for the public to see a different perspective based around this highly controversial subject, hypnosis, hypnotherapy, stage hypnosis, and the dangers of hypnosis, and who better to tell the story than someone with firsthand experience, an expert in his own field, even though he has now completely withdrawn from this profession."

Dr. Wheeler asks some interesting questions.

"What real knowledge does the hypnotherapist have? What training has he or she undergone with regards to psychology and psychiatry? But above all, this person who is about to hypnotise you, to take control and influence your mind, do they really know what they are doing? How can they?

Even if they were the worlds most highly recognised doctor of psychology or professor of psychiatry, science and the medical profession openly admit they don't know what the mind is. The brain, yes, and this organ, the brain is so highly complex, but the mind can't even be seen or touched, it is something invisible, abstract, intangible, something from the invisible world, part of our consciousness."

Hypnotherapists will often tell people that watching television, driving a car and fishing, produce trance like states of consciousness within the mind. So hypnotism, they say, is completely natural. Dr. Wheeler disagrees

"The truth is that yes, all these activities previously mentioned, watching television, driving a car and fishing, can and do produce trance like states of consciousness within the mind. But this is not true hypnosis.

True hypnosis is when another person deliberately attempts to alter your own state of consciousness, taking you from your natural trance like state of mind, into a deeper hypnotic state of consciousness, so that in turn, they can influence your thoughts and feelings - through suggestions of their own choosing!

The majority of hypnotists and hypnotherapists will also tell you, "You can't be hypnotised against your will" and secondly,"You would not fundamentally do anything that would contradict your own moral values or ethics."

The truth is- most people can be hypnotised against their own will, and some people can be made to do anything.

You can be hypnotised against your will, and with a highly skilled operator, they could get you to do anything! and that's scary.

It isn't that all hypnotists are liars. It is that the majority of them are not even aware of the power they wield themselves. Many hypnotherapists wouldn't know how to hypnotise someone against their will, even though at times they are actually doing it, or how to get someone to carry out an act that in normal life circumstances they wouldn't perform. However, many stage hypnotist know how to do these things, but generally they remain secretive about their profession."

It seems to me that hypnotism, with its roots in ancient Egypt, touches the most intimate area of a human being. In the world in which we live, pages of data are being constantly gathered about us. Governments would like that data all in one place to access it for their own purposes. The one place of privacy we have left is our mind. The very place hypnotism wants to access and alter.

"Hypnosis is a form of trespass upon another's consciousness. Repeated hypnosis, and the negative effects it produces, can eventually derange the brain cells.

Hypnotism has been used by physicians in minor operations as a sort of psychical chloroform for persons who might be endangered by an anaesthetic. But a hypnotic state is harmful to those often subjected to it; a negative psychological effect ensues that in time deranges the brain cells. Hypnotism is trespass into the territory of another's consciousness."

(Autobiography of a Yogi by Paramahansa Yogananda)

Dr. Wheeler also advises against the dangers of subjecting ourselves to hypnotism.

"If another person's will is continually imposed upon you via hypnotic techniques, that energy from their will, forcing control over your mind or bodily functions, only hammers in another nail to your own bondage of being a slave to your senses, and hinders you from becoming a master of yourself. Also, there are other unconscious suggestions that are entering your subconscious that you are not even aware of."

Am I making too much out of what's meant to be a bit of fun? Is it too much to suggest a little trance of hypnotism could cause serious harm? One final time I quote Dr. Wheeler, who is a trained and very experienced hypnotherpist, thankfully one who has turned his back on the practice.

"Once at a Butlin's holiday camp, right at the start of a show I dropped this man into instant trance. A few minutes later I said, "Wakey wakey, what are you doing down there lying on the floor?"

The young man, around the age of 30, leapt to his feet, turned to the person next to him, and put his hands around the person's throat in an attempt to strangle him! I quickly intervened with the word "Sleep", and the subject fell back to the floor in a trance. I quickly gave suggestions of inner confidence, ego hypnosis causing psychosisboosting, and suggestions of peace-of-mind and well-being. I then awoke him and he returned back to the audience. All this happened within a few minutes, the audience didn't really know what was happening and I had a show to perform. Unfortunately the story doesn't end there. Immediately after I had finished the show there were further problems with this individual. He had turned insane, and was acting like a madman thinking he was a soldier. He was out to kill, and not to be captured.

Due to the strong emotional content I would rather not recall this story in detail, but will say that it was a very frightening experience for myself and the other people involved. Luck being on my side the situation was resolved, and the young man concerned spent the night in a local hospital."

I'm not saying in all of this, that hypnotism isn't effective - it certainly does bring change. A lady I know went to see a hypnotist because she was addicted to eating chocolate. Hypnotism was effective in that she can't eat chocolate anymore. If she puts it near her mouth she feels she wants to vomit. My point is that someone else has controlled, and continues to control, this lady.

She needs to decide whether to eat chocolate or not. Not have her thoughts tapped into and altered by another human being. She may not eat chocolate anymore, but what else has she opened herself up to?

The main problem with most 'alternative therapies' is their source. If we are being asked to engage in something that promises healing or touches our spirit, its source must be Jesus Christ. If the root or source is anything else, it allows spiritual toxins into the centre of our being.

Modern medicine has its roots in Christianity - that's why many hospitals are named after Christian saints. By contrast, hypnotism, the ancient art of mind alteration, with its roots in ancient Egypt, does not have its source in Christ. I believe it is a spiritual toxin we need to avoid or be cleansed from.

Remember the life pattern we looked at? Our thoughts ultimately dictate our destiny. Should we really give anyone but Jesus control over our mind?

Healing of the family tree and healing of the memories.

In the 1980's there was an explosion in the Christian world of '*Healing of the memories*' teaching and ministry. There were also books on healing the family tree and generational healing. A part of this ministry is regression to childhood. This is actually a technique of hypnosis, which is very dangerous. The are strict laws in the UK about the practice of hypnotic regression.

God can heal us everywhere we hurt and he doesn't use hypnotic regression. If we go back to my story about the effects of pornography, when I was prayed with, Jesus wiped my memory of the negative images. There was no trance and no regression. I just felt my head burning and from that moment the past was dealt with supernaturally.

Sometimes, the regression teaching begins with things like forgiveness, which, I hope I have shown, is clearly in accord with the Bible and the teaching of Jesus. But then they mix in going back over and over your life, back to childhood, trying to think of people to forgive. Then they get into healing every month since we were conceived and mix hypnotic regression with the command to forgive.

You do not need to sit and agonise over the possibility that you missed forgiving someone. The Holy Spirit will bring to mind the things we need to do. If we're really concerned, we should ask the Holy Spirit to bring to mind anyone we need to forgive. If no one comes to mind, we don't need to worry. We do not need to constantly rake over the past. What will set us free is doing the right thing from today.

I personally know people who have been greatly troubled by demonic attacks as a result of ministry by 'deliverance ministries' who use regression and family tree techniques. **We do not need to repent on behalf of our family or our ancestors or our tribe.** God will only ever hold us accountable for our own actions. Nor will he forgive any ancestor of ours, if we 'repent on their behalf'.

"The soul who sins is the one who will die. The son will not share the guilt of the father, nor will the father share the guilt of the son. The righteousness of the righteous man will be credited to him, and the wickedness of the wicked will be charged against him. But if a wicked man turns away from all the sins he has committed and keeps all my decrees and does what is just and right, he will surely live; he will not die. None of the offences he has committed will be remembered against him. Because of the righteous things he has done, he will live."

(Ezekiel 18: 20 - 22)

It is true that, where there has been a family feud, we could take some action to put things right and restore a relationship. But we cannot change what others have done in the past, only what we do today and in the future.

Most of these memory and family tree ministries will have no idea that they are engaging in hypnotism. They will believe that because they 'involve Jesus' and do it 'prayerfully' it is OK. You will not find healing of the memories or healing of the family tree anywhere in the Bible. I believe it was a 1980's psuedo-Christian 'fad', not rooted in scripture and was based on hypnosis techniques, mingled with aspects of Christianity and sometimes even a bit of witchcraft. I would recommend you steer well clear of anyone wanting you to 'relax and go back to your childhood'.

Obviously, I'm not saying there's anything wrong with chatting over bad stuff that happened when we were little. We all need a friend to counsel us occasionally. Sometimes, just talking about stuff that happened in the past helps us process things and find resolution. However, once we start being told to close our eyes and relax and to '*go back*' - even if it's said to be '*with Jesus*', we should stop and walk away. We will end up giving control of our mind to someone else. However well intentioned they may be, this can often lead to trouble later. In reality they have no idea what they are doing, because they cannot understand the mind or know what it is - no one does, except Jesus.

We need to detox our thoughts. As some of you are reading this, I believe God is also showing you other ways that you need to detox your thoughts. I pray that from this day, your thoughts may be sweet and full of peace. That you will be confident that the God of heaven loves you just as you are, and loves you too much to leave you just as you are.

I am not what I should be. I'm not what I could be. But by the grace of God, I am not what I was. Day by day, Jesus Christ is changing me into his likeness. It's a journey we are all called to.

[Due to the present climate of the issuing of many lawsuits in the hypnosis community I am required to mention that the intentions of this book are spiritual teaching and no libel, either professional or personal, is intended to any person or organisation.]

3. Detox your words

Your words are powerful. If you've ever been subjected to sincere praise or stinging criticism - or both - you know words are powerful. The Bible says, "Death and life are in the power of the tongue..." (Proverbs 18:21) When God created the world, he used words. God said 'Let there be light' and there was light. You are created in God's image. If God's words carry creative power, so do yours. What comes out of your mouth has power in the spiritual realm. Things born in the spirit, will eventually manifest in the 'flesh'. Your words will give birth to good or evil, blessing or curse.

Jesus told his followers that they could move mountains by the power of their words.

> "I say to you, whoever says to this mountain, 'Be removed and be cast into the sea,' and does not doubt in his heart, but believes that those things he says will be done, he will have whatever he says."
> (Mark 11:23)

The telling phrase here is, '*he will have whatever he says*'. What comes out of our mouth is what we end up with.

In the book of Numbers, chapter 13, we find the story of the children of Israel when they were in the wilderness. They come to the border with the Promised Land - their planned destination. Moses, at God's instruction, sends some men to spy out the land to see if they can take it. On their return, all the spies agreed it was a great place.

"We went to the land where you sent us. It truly flows with milk and honey, and this is its fruit." They had brought back samples of the goodness of the land. But there the unanimous agreement ended. The majority saw problems in taking the land.

"Nevertheless the people who dwell in the land are strong; the cities are fortified and very large; moreover we saw the descendants of Anak [giants] there."

Now fear came out of their mouth. They saw the land was good but they said there were insurmountable problems in taking the land. Only two men disagreed - Caleb and Joshua.

"Then Caleb quieted the people before Moses, and said, "Let us go up at once and take possession, for we are well able to overcome it." But the men who had gone up with him said, "We are not able to go up against the people, for they are stronger than we." And they gave the children of Israel a bad report of the land which they had spied out, saying, "The land through which we have gone as spies is a land that devours its inhabitants, and all the people whom we saw in it are men of great stature. There we saw the giants (the descendants of Anak came from the giants); and we were like grasshoppers in our own sight, and so we were in their sight.'"

(Numbers 13:25-33)

The Bible says, that as a man thinks in his heart, so is he. (Proverbs 23:7) The majority in this story saw themselves a small and powerless.

"...we were like grasshoppers in our own sight." Only Joshua and Caleb said they could take the land that God had promised them.

God's judgement on this dispute is very informative. God said that everyone was going to get... *what they said.* Those who *said* we will die if we try to take the land, would die. But those who *said*, 'we can take the land' - Joshua and Caleb - were the only members of that group who finally entered the Promised Land.

"Say to them, 'As I live,' says the LORD, 'just as you have spoken in My hearing, so I will do to you:"

(Numbers 14:28)

It's consistent with Jesus' teaching in Mark 11:23, 'he shall have whatever he says'.

So our words are powerful. Our words are like seeds. When Jesus told the parable of the sower, he explained, "The sower sows the word." (Mark 4:14) So the seeds in this parable are the words coming out of our mouth. Jesus also said that this was the key parable. If you don't get this one, you can't understand any parable.

> "And He said to them, "Do you not understand this parable? How then will you understand all the parables?"
>
> (Mark 4:13)

What we sow is what we reap. Every day seeds of power are dropping from our lips. Every word will have a harvest for good or ill. That's why Jesus said he would judge our words.

> "But I tell you that men will have to give account on the day of judgement for every careless word they have spoken."
>
> (Matthew 12:36, NIV)

We need to be careful what comes out of our mouth. Our words will grow into reality. Our thoughts create our words and then our words create our actions.

Have you ever noticed how you start thinking about buying some gadget, some particular item of clothing or a pair of shoes? Next you start talking about them. You tell your friends you're thinking about this or that. Eventually you end up going out to buy the thing. See the progression - thoughts, words, actions.

If you are constantly talking about sickness and trouble with your mouth, you are sowing the seeds of those things happening around you or to you. If you walk around saying all the time, 'Well, it always goes wrong for me. Other people have good stuff happen, but it always goes wrong for me.' You're thinking negatively. You're speaking negatively. You're depressing to be around, quite frankly. Worse still, a lot of that bad stuff will happen to you because you've got real faith for it.

The Bible says, "...faith comes by hearing..." (Romans 10:17) If you're hearing yourself saying a lot of negative stuff, day in and day out, those seeds dropping from your mouth are going to be watered by your faith and they are going to sprout into reality.

But what if you were to start reading the Bible and seeing what God says about you? You could start thinking and saying some good stuff. Here's a few thoughts God has about you.

> "For I know the plans I have for you," declares the LORD, "plans to prosper you and not to harm you, plans to give you hope and a future."
>
> (Jeremiah 29:11, NIV)

> "Goodness and mercy shall follow [you] all the days of [your] life."
>
> (Psalm 23:6)

"God... gives you power to get wealth..."
(Deuteronomy 8:18)

"...by his wounds we are healed."
(Isaiah 53:5)

"No evil shall befall you, Nor shall any plague come near your dwelling;"
(Psalms 91:10)

"Blessed be the Lord, Who daily loads us with benefits."
(Psalm 68:19)

"Bless the LORD, O my soul, And forget not all His benefits: Who forgives all your iniquities, Who heals all your diseases, Who redeems your life from destruction, Who crowns you with loving kindness and tender mercies, Who satisfies your mouth with good things, So that your youth is renewed like the eagle's."
(Psalm 103:2-5)

We need to detox our words. We need to get God's word into our head and into our heart. We need to read it, think about it, speak it out of our mouth and water those seeds with faith, so that those things we say will begin to happen to us. It's not so much 'what you *see* is what you get', as 'what you *say* is what you get'. You can be sure that what you say today, you'll be doing tomorrow.

It is very easy to let defeat and negative words fall from your lips. It takes practice to get God's words to come out of your mouth. Take time today to listen to yourself. How many negative things are coming out of your mouth? How many positive statements? Which are in the majority? If you're speaking words like 'I am sick to death...' all the time, you need to detox your words. If you don't, you are sowing the seeds of sickness and death.

A prayer

Jesus,

Help me to stop speaking so negatively.

Take the word '*can't*' out of my vocabulary.

Holy Spirit, help me to put God's word into my mind and into my heart, for out of the heart the mouth speaks.

I thank you that you have plans to prosper me. I thank you that goodness and mercy will follow me all the days of my life. I thank you that by the wounds of Jesus, I am healed.

I thank you that you have given me power to get wealth. May I use it for good. Thank you that no evil shall before me. Thank you for loading me with benefits every day.

Amen.

4. Detox your actions

Last night, I read a story of how two men are assisting the police with their enquiries. One is in a critical state in intensive care after being allegedly assaulted by his neighbour. The picture showed a car that had been driven through the neighbour's garden wall on purpose. It was a dispute about parking. Other neighbours described both families as lovely people and said these actions were 'totally out of character'. The street was described as a 'quiet street'.

We've already seen that actions spring from the words we speak. Words spring from our thoughts. However, even if we have made the mistake of thinking and saying toxic things, when the moment of action comes, we still have a choice. We can stop things right there. It's a lot easier to stop negative actions at the thought stage but if we've let it get to the action stage, we can stop before we act.

When we come to a decision that will definitely change things, we should always sleep on it at least one night. This is not procrastination. It's a cooling off period. Cooling off periods are now a legal requirement of all insurance and credit contracts in the UK. This is so we can undo a bad decision.

If you are acting in anger and rage, you really need to stop and work through the roots of your anger. It is almost certainly not the issue you are focussed on. It's normally something else, something unresolved from your past which you are now projecting onto the current situation.

The film '*The Weatherman*', starring Nicholas Cage, is a dark film. It deals with the main character's inner struggles with his life - his marriage breakdown, his teenage children's struggles, his relationship with his dying father and his wife's new boyfriend. He considers murdering the boyfriend for a brief moment. On a trip to the hospital with his sick father, played by Michael Caine, he talks with his father about difficult decisions. His father offers him some advice. "The hard thing to do and the right thing to do are often the same thing." Isn't that true?

Good character is revealed in big events but it is formed in small ones. Doing the right thing today will pay dividends tomorrow. Doing the right thing today makes us walk in success tomorrow. Doing the right thing establishes a reputation.

Jesus told a story and asked a question. "What do you think? There was a man who had two sons. He went to the first and said, 'Son, go and work today in the vineyard.'

'I will not,' he answered, but later he changed his mind and went.

Then the father went to the other son and said the same thing. He answered, 'I will, sir,' but he did not go. Which of the two did what his father wanted?"

"The first," they answered. Jesus said to them, "I tell you the truth, the tax collectors and the prostitutes are entering the kingdom of God ahead of you."

(Matthew 21:28-31, NIV)

Whatever you did in the past, continually doing the right thing from now on will change the course of your life. In the early days of IBM, legend has it, a man was developing a new computer system. He made some wrong decisions and took some wrong actions. With the press of a single button he lost the company £10,000. He was called into the managers office. "I suppose I'm fired", he said. "Fired?" said his boss. "No way! I've just spent £10,000 training you to do the right thing!" We may have done the wrong thing in the past but if we will learn from our past mistakes and do the right thing from today, it will change our life for the better.

Don't burn your bridges.
The world is a very small place. We are almost certainly going to meet people again. Several years ago, I was on a mission to Africa. I had

been on mission in Rwanda for two weeks and I was tired. But before I returned home, I had to do another week of mission in a remote area of Uganda. It was miles from civilisation or a tarmac road. I would be preaching every day for a week. Halfway through this mission, I was really longing to go home. The people of that village gave us the very best of everything they had. They didn't have much but what they had they gave. We stayed in the only house for a hundred miles that had a flush toilet. I was very thankful for that.

However, we were cooking for ourselves. There were three of us and a camping stove. So catering was not our strong point. The beds had bedbugs and we were being bitten every night while we tried to sleep. We also had a full day's journey, along muddy roads, to get back to the city before we left for home.

On the last night, I told the Archdeacon we were working with, that we would have to leave early in the morning. 'Yes', he said. He wanted a meeting in the morning but I knew that would lead to long repetitive speeches of thanks that, as far as I was concerned were totally unnecessary. I tried to put him off. During the night there was torrential rain. The bus couldn't reach our house at the top of a muddy hill. So we had to carry all our belongings for half a mile, walking through thick mud. We arrived at the bottom of the hill looking like refugees from a war. Our shoes were covered with think mud and our trousers had muddy wet stains up to our knees.

Then I got a message that the Archdeacon had arranged a communion service at the church and was waiting for us. The church was another half-mile walk in thick mud.

I'm afraid I 'lost it'. I totally refused to walk to the church for a communion service. A messenger was sent to tell the Archdeacon I was not coming. A message came back that, 'The Lord's table is set and the Archdeacon is waiting'. I reasoned with myself that it would obviously upset this man if I didn't go but on the other hand, after today, I would never see him again. So I stubbornly refused to go. I felt bad, as in the end, one of my team went on my behalf, so I still had to wait to go home. As we arrived home in the UK, I felt I hadn't done the right thing but was sure I'd never meet the Archdeacon again.

Six months later, the Archdeacon was given a grant to visit the UK. Inevitably, he arrived in the UK and after a few phone calls, he was sat in my front room and I was eating humble pie with a large spoon. Fortunately for me, he was very gracious. For the cost of a bit of grace and patience - and an hour or two of my time - I could have done the right thing. OK, it wasn't the end of the world but it makes the point that the world is a small place and we are probably going to meet people again, however fleeting our original meeting. So don't burn your bridges. As far as it depends on you, do the right thing even if the right thing is also the hard thing to do.

Let your 'Yes be Yes'
Isn't it really irritating when people agree to do something for you and then they don't deliver. Or isn't irritating when people agree they won't do something and then they do. Nobody wants to be around people who say one thing and do another.

Sometimes, because we want people to like us, we agree to do something and then deeply regret saying yes. But if we said yes, we should do what we say. It's better to say 'No' if we mean 'No'. People will actually appreciate you more if you say 'No' when you mean 'no' because then they will know where they stand with you. Saying one thing and doing the opposite is very frustrating for those around you.

Jesus said, "Let your 'Yes' be 'Yes,' and your 'No,' 'No.' For whatever is more than these is from the evil one."
(Matthew 5:37)

Some people I know, who are divorced, say

that one of the key problems was that they could never believe anything their spouse said. Often we tell people what we think they want to hear, with no intention of delivering on the agreement. This sort of behaviour poisons relationships because it seriously undermines trust. Trust is the lubricant of relationships and negotiations. It is much better to get a reputation as someone who will often say 'No' but if he says 'Yes' he means it, rather than someone whose word is worthless.

Don't confuse your 'who' with your 'do'.

We need to know who we are in Jesus. The Bible tells us that when we receive Jesus Christ into our heart and put him first, that we are a new creation.

> "Therefore, if anyone is in Christ, he is a new creation; old things have passed away; behold, all things have become new."
> (2 Corinthians 5:17)

If we are a new creation in Jesus, we must not let our previous life determine who we are. We may do things wrong occasionally, but who we are is now determined by our relationship with Jesus.

If we have a chaotic past, if we are struggling to overcome addictions or if we are trying to make the best of a mess, we may sometimes do things that are not right. Detoxing our life is really a lifelong task. As I sometimes tell my wife, 'I'm an oil painting not a photograph. God hasn't finished with me yet'.

Who I am is a child of God, reconciled to the Father, being transformed daily by the Holy Spirit. *What I do* is sometimes make mistakes or wrong decisions. Sometimes I discover I haven't learnt God's latest lesson yet. But *who I am* doesn't change or become negated because I *do* some stuff that is wrong occasionally. I'm a work in progress.

Now, if I am in Christ and a new creation, I really shouldn't be going round and round the same circle making the same mistakes again and again. Repeatedly doing the same thing over and over again and expecting a different outcome is really insanity. We reap what we sow. If you keep doing what you've been doing, you will keep getting what you've been getting. But if you *do* the wrong thing occasionally then don't think that *who you are* is necessarily negated. God is the God of restoration. Don't confuse your '*who*' with your '*do*'

Don't get revenge.

I heard a story recently of a man who keeps a box of golf balls in his car. If someone cuts him up in traffic, he gets in front of them and then opens his sunroof and starts throwing golf balls out of the sunroof so they hit the other guy's car. It sounds amusing but think about it for a moment. Have you ever taken revenge on someone and felt good about yourself afterwards? It's not a good feeling at all because we've usually overdone it or hurt someone quite badly.

Really, a desire to get revenge shows that we have poison deep within our heart. Jesus tells us,

> "A good tree does not bear bad fruit, nor does a bad tree bear good fruit. For every tree is known by its own fruit. For men do not gather figs from thorns, nor do they gather grapes from a bramble bush. A good man out of the good treasure of his heart brings forth good; and an evil man out of the evil treasure of his heart brings forth evil. For out of the abundance of the heart his mouth speaks."
>
> (Luke 6:43-45)

If we want to live like Jesus and be in peace we need to detox our actions. We need to check the source of our actions. Are we acting from bitterness, hurt or pride? Or are we acting out of a good heart? Of course, most of us feel like killing certain people at times. They make us so angry. But we should really think about what we actually do because our repeated actions will form our habits, which in turn will form our character. The Bible teaches an alternative lifestyle when it comes to actions.

"Repay no one evil for evil. Have regard for good things in the sight of all men. If it is possible, as much as depends on you, live peaceably with all men. Beloved, do not avenge yourselves, but rather give place to wrath; for it is written, "Vengeance is Mine, I will repay," says the Lord. Therefore "If your enemy is hungry, feed him; If he is thirsty, give him a drink; For in so doing you will heap coals of fire on his head." Do not be overcome by evil, but overcome evil with good."

(Romans 12:17-21)

I have a friend who was verbally attacked and accused by people in the church. The attack was unprovoked and unjust. The victim of the attack felt very hurt and angry. But what was the right thing to do? My friend prayed for wisdom to know how to respond. She then sent her attackers a substantial financial gift for their ministry. The attackers were silenced and their attitude changed overnight. The venom of their attacks evaporated. My friend was completely set free because she acted in a godly way. The perpetrators were silenced because they had 'coals of fire heaped on their head.'

What will they say at your funeral?
In Charles Dicken's '*A Christmas Carol*',
Scrooge is shocked into action when the spirit of
'Christmas to come' shows him his own funeral.
It's a miserable affair and no one has a good word
to say about him.

But what about your funeral? What will be
said there? Why don't you write the speech you
want made at your funeral and then work out
what you will have to do to cause someone to
make that speech?

Then you will have a list of actions you need
to take to have a successful life.

When you wake up in the morning you have
a clean sheet of paper for the day ahead. Your
actions will make the difference. The Bible says
that God's mercies are new every morning.

> "Through the LORD'S mercies we are
> not consumed, because His compassions
> fail not. They are new every morning; Great
> is Your faithfulness."

(Lamentations 3:22, 23)

I'm so glad his mercies are new every morning
because I used up all yesterdays. God's word will
always tell us how to act.

> "He has showed you, O man, what is
> good. And what does the LORD require of
> you? To act justly and to love mercy and to

walk humbly with your God."

(Micah 6:8, NIV)

There are basically two types of action you can take today - you can *repair* or *prepare*. People who spend their lives repairing are always trying to put right what they did wrong yesterday. People who are preparing are making sure they live in success tomorrow.

When our son was alive, one of the funniest things he ever did was to put some red food colouring into his rice pudding. He stirred in the colour clockwise but was disappointed that it turned his pudding pink. He began stirring his pudding anticlockwise to undo the action but was horrified when his pudding stayed pink. You can't change the past but you can determine your future. Next time you have rice pudding you can leave out the colouring.

What one action can you do today that would change your life for the better? What one action can you do this week that will make a real change? What one action can you do this year to make a difference to your life? In the Bible we read in several places that often just one thing is needed.

"Now it happened as they went that He entered a certain village; and a certain woman named Martha welcomed Him into her house. And she had a sister called Mary, who also sat at Jesus' feet and heard His word. But Martha was distracted with much serving, and she approached Him and said, "Lord, do You not care that my sister has left me to serve alone? Therefore tell her to help me." And Jesus answered and said to her, "Martha, Martha, you are worried and troubled about many things. But *one thing* is needed, and Mary has chosen that good part, which will not be taken away from her."

(Luke 10:38-42).

Mary decided that the one thing that was needed was to listen to the words of Jesus. Maybe that's the one thing you should do right now that will bring real change and real peace to your life. You could start listening to Jesus. You can read his words in the gospels and then think about them. As you meditate on what he says you will be listening to him. This one thing could change the course of your life.

In another meeting, Jesus was speaking to someone who was very rich. The rich young man wanted to know what he had to do to inherit eternal life.

Jesus said to him, "You know the commandments: 'Do not commit adultery, Do not murder, Do not steal, Do not bear false witness, Do not defraud, Honour your father and your mother.'"

And he answered and said to Him, "Teacher, all these things I have kept from my youth." Then Jesus, looking at him, loved him, and said to him, "*One thing* you lack: Go your way, sell whatever you have and give to the poor, and you will have treasure in heaven; and come, take up the cross, and follow Me."
(Mark 10:19-21).

The one thing this rich man needed to do was to put God before his riches. He'd done all the 'right things' for all his life. But for him the one thing he needed to do was to start giving to the poor. Maybe that's the one thing you need to do to make a real change.

Our work in RSVP is all about giving. I love to give. It took me a long time to learn, but living a life of giving is true freedom. The Bible tells us that when we give to the poor, God sees it and counts it as a debt he owes to us. He will pay us back for all our giving to the poor.

"He who has pity on the poor lends to the LORD, And He will pay back what he has given."
(Proverbs 19:17)

Some people just need to let go of the past and

forgive themselves. Saint Paul had previously spent his time persecuting Christians and putting them to death. The Bible tells us he stood and watched as Stephen, the first martyr, was stoned to death. The execution was almost certainly arranged by Paul. No doubt this could have haunted him once he became a Christian. But did he let that hold him back?

He wrote to the believers at Philippi,

"...*one thing* I do: Forgetting what is behind and straining towards what is ahead, I press on towards the goal to win the prize for which God has called me heavenwards in Christ Jesus."
(Philippians 3:13, 14)

Maybe forgetting what's past is the one action you could take that would set the course for this year. If this is true for you, I pray for 'holy amnesia' in the things you need to forget.

Others need to spend time in God's presence. They need a personal encounter with Jesus. David wrote in the Psalms,

"*One thing* I have desired of the LORD, that will I seek: That I may dwell in the house of the LORD all the days of my life, to behold the beauty of the LORD, and to inquire in His temple."
(Psalms 27:4).

I am convinced that whatever situation you are facing today, there is *one right thing* you could do today that will change your life. Taking the right action over and over will start to detox your actions and form some good habits.

5. Detox your habits

In the Anglican Church I often feel that if we do something twice, we have established a tradition and people will begin to say, 'But we've always done it that way.' We don't want to get ourselves in a rut, but forming habits can be a great strength if they are the right habits. Drug addicts talk of needing so much money a day to 'feed their habit'. Bad habits will control us. Good habits will set us free and keep us safe.

One of the most helpful things I ever did was a little exercise given to me by Professor Martin Saunders from America. He suggested to a group of us that we should imagine for a moment that we are Satan. And then we should write down the strategy we would use to destroy our personal life and ministry. For me, it was almost immediate. I could see that if Satan attacked me in three particular areas, every day, I would soon fall.

The second part of the exercise was to write down some policies or procedures that I would follow to protect myself from such a strategy. I could clearly see that I was weakest when I travelled alone. From that day, I have rarely travelled alone when going to speaking engagements. I also put in place other procedures to protect myself.

Bad habits run a high risk of becoming addictions. We sometimes think that we could stop bad habits anytime we want. When we think that, we are usually already addicted. I am told that if you drop a frog into boiling water, it will jump straight out again because of the shock. However, if you put a frog in cold water and slowly bring it to the boil, it will sit there and allow itself to be slowly poached to death without even noticing what's happening. Bad habits turn into addictions gradually, almost imperceptibly. They subtly begin to control our life.

The man who drinks a couple of times to drown his sorrows, one day finds himself unable to remember the last day he didn't drink and his waking thoughts are about what time he can start drinking today. An addiction is anything that controls us, anything we can't get through the day without getting our fix of.

So how do we develop good habits? Firstly, good habits do not come naturally, we have to work to establish them and we need God's help. It is also possible to begin to develop good habits while we still have some bad ones - it's often a transition. Here are a few good habits I have developed over the years that I have found helpful.

Solitude brings perspective.
When things get hard, heated or confusing, take some time out. Walk away from the situation and see it from a distance. It may annoy the other people involved, but it is usually the right thing to do. Jesus did it.

> "Now in the morning, having risen a long while before daylight, He went out and departed to a solitary place; and there He prayed. And Simon and those who were with Him searched for Him. When they found Him, they said to Him, "Everyone is looking for You." But He said to them, "Let us go into the next towns, that I may preach there also, because for this purpose I have come forth.""

(Mark 1:35-38)

I love this account of Jesus' life. 'Everyone is looking for you!' the disciples tell Jesus. You can imagine the modern equivalent - 'You have several urgent e-mails, they have left several voice-mails, they keep phoning for you. Where have you been?'

But Jesus was away early in the morning getting perspective, being with his Father. Then the other thing I really like, far from rushing back to deal with the confusion, he says 'Let's go somewhere else. I have a purpose to fulfil.' Solitude keeps us on track. It helps us to see the bigger picture of our life. Parents with young children should go away without them at least once a year. But they should also have a day away on their own once in a while.

God the builder - can he fix it? Yes he can!
Another habit I am still developing is going to God as soon as it stops working. When things come to a stalemate, go to God. I usually say to Him, 'God, I have done everything I know to do but it's not working. Will you please help me? Show me the key to this situation. Your word says, 'If any of you lacks wisdom, let him ask of God, who gives to all liberally and without finding fault, and it will be given to him. (James 1:5) So right now, I receive your wisdom on the matter.' Then I stop the snowball thinking I mentioned earlier and get on with my life. Every time I have done this, suddenly, an idea comes into my head that resolves the problem. I believe that is God giving me the wisdom to get a breakthrough.

Put God first, first.

Still another thing we should do, as a habit, is to put God first. He should be first in everything. How do we do that? Well God should be first - F.I.R.S.T. God should be first in our:

Finances

Interests

Relationships

Schedule

Troubles

God should be first in our *finances*. Sometimes the last part of a person to get saved is his pocket. But if God is not Lord *of* all, he is not Lord *at* all. When Jesus went to the house of Zacceus, his money was the first thing it affected. Some people balk at giving God ten percent of their income. But I think Jesus taught us that God requires one hundred percent of all we have. The fact that he is usually happy for us to keep ninety percent is a bonus and a privilege.

God should be first in our *interests*. What we spend our time doing and thinking about needs to come under God's control.

God should be first in our *relationships*. People we spend time with affect our life and who we become. Are our relationships pleasing to God?

God should be first in our *schedule*. How do we spend our time? Are we too busy or are we too lazy? God calls us to live a balanced life. Running round like a headless chicken without real purpose will send us to an early grave. Laying on the sofa all day watching daytime TV will bring us to the same place. Let God rule in your schedule.

God should be first in our *troubles*. Trouble may come but it must not overcome. We should put God first when trouble comes and follow his strategy to get a breakthrough that releases us from trouble.

You can do anything if you give it an hour a day.

Several people have asked me over the years, 'How have you found time to write so many books?' I can tell you that everyone who has asked me that question could write better books than me. They have a lot to say to the world, but they just never get round to starting. Or they start but don't finish.

All my books were written by giving at least one hour a day to the task. It's best for me if I can give the first hour of the day to it. Once I get into the flow, I try and get a whole morning or even a day to make progress. It becomes the most important thing in my day and I do it around all the other things I have to do.

As I write this chapter, I am on a mission in Rwanda. It's a busy trip but I have taken a day out of the schedule to make some progress on this book. I have borrowed a laptop and I'm sitting in the grounds of the hotel tapping away at the keyboard. Waiters are on hand to supply me with coffee.

My point here is that if you give anything one hour a day, you will become accomplished. You can learn a musical instrument, a foreign language, an accounting system - whatever you want. You can do it all, if you give it an hour a day. You just need to be disciplined and make what you do a habit.

Make time for positive relationships.
Something else that will change your life is pursuing relationships of influence. If you spend all your time with negative people, you will tend to become negative. Some people are so negative, if they touched your car battery they would drain all the power out of it. Others are so narrow minded they can look through a keyhole with both eyes. You need to get with some positive people - people of influence and inspiration. Most people are happy to do lunch with you once in a while. Ask them.

Every six weeks or so, I take a day out of my schedule to be with my friend Martin Garner. We are both busy people but we know that this habit reaps rewards. We meet at a lake which is about half way between our homes. We both have a two hour drive to meet there. We have coffee and talk. We walk by the lake. Martin is one of the Britain's authorities on birds, so as we walk he shows me things I would never notice on my own. We go for lunch and talk some more. We inspire and encourage each other. We make plans. I really look forward to these days.

Once a year, I have the privilege of spending three days with a group of evangelists. This retreat is a top priority for me. I always come back challenged, equipped, rested and inspired. I never see spending time with positive people as a waste of time. It's always a good use of my time.

Spend time with your spouse.
Last year, Hazel and I were thinking we needed to take more exercise. We wanted to do something together. We took up badminton on Saturday mornings and we protect that time from interruptions. It's sacred space. It enables us to spend time together. We don't take the game too seriously - its about being together and taking exercise. Often we don't even bother to keep the score, we just thrash the shuttlecock at each other.

When the children were little it was hard to find time to be alone. But now they've grown up its a lot easier. But we still have to make time for each other. If we don't invest in our marriage we may find that when the children have flown the nest, we are left living with a stranger. The Bible says, "May you rejoice in the wife of your youth." (Proverbs 5:18, NIV)

As you can see, on their own, these are not earth shattering activities. But together, as a group of good habits, they begin to build a detoxed lifestyle that is creative rather than destructive.

If you begin to do good stuff on purpose and increase the amount of good habits you form, you will eventually push out the bad habits because you won't have time for them. The saying that 'the Devil makes work for idle hands' is true. Get busy forming some good habits. Start doing something different today.

6. Detox your character

Anything minus integrity equals zero. I have seen people, even people in the church, bend the rules a little. They act without integrity for short term gain. As I look around now, I can't see any of them. They've long gone. All their little schemes amounted to nothing. Their influence has evaporated without a trace.

Some people have a vague sense of integrity but they can also be bought for a price. This undermines their integrity.

A lady was on a plane when a well dressed business man sat in the seat next to her. As they chatted he made an indecent proposal. He said he would pay her £1,000,000 if she would spend the night and sleep with him. At first she was shocked. But as they came in to land she asked if he was serious. He said he was. They arranged the time and the place. They agreed all the other arrangements. Then the man said, "All is agreed. I just want to make one final change. The price is actually £10." The lady got really angry. "What do you think I am?" She demanded. The man replied, "What you are has already been established. We are just haggling about the price."

We should be faithful to who we are regardless of bribes. There will always be temptations to compromise with the devil.

Jesus said "He who is faithful in what is least is faithful also in much; and he who is unjust in what is least is unjust also in much."

(Luke 16:10)

If we repeatedly do the right thing in small matters, God will be able to trust us with bigger things. But if we are corrupt in small matters, we will be corrupt if trusted with more.

I always find it interesting to read of people who win the national lottery and go to pieces once they get the money. Money will only magnify what is already in your heart. If you are living on benefits or the minimum wage, your opportunities to sin are limited. But if you are suddenly given millions of pounds, your options are multiplied. Money only magnifies what is already in your heart. If you have integrity when you are poor, you will have integrity when you become rich.

David was anointed to be king over Israel. But there was a long delay between receiving the anointing and receiving the crown. In the meantime God was watching his heart. God will usually test us with a smaller and more difficult version of what he has called us to, while we are in transition. The purpose of this test is to develop our character.

King Saul wanted to kill David because he saw him as a threat to his throne. So David had the *anointing* to be king but not the *crown*. In addition to that, he now had a death threat hanging over his life. It is at this difficult time that David's test of character arrives.

> "And everyone who was in distress, everyone who was in debt, and everyone who was discontented gathered to him. So he became captain over them. And there were about four hundred men with him."
> (1 Samuel 22:2)

As if life wasn't hard enough, he now finds that he has become *king of the depressed people*. This sounds like one of the most difficult groups of people you could ever find yourself leader of. But David knew the principle of being faithful with little so that God will give us more.

As the story unfolds David is faithful with the depressed people and eventually, after many trials, he steps into the palace and wears the crown. He not only needed the anointing - that would only get him into the palace - he needed the character to keep him there. Your charisma or anointing may get you through the door, but you will need to have developed your character in order to stay there.

Most leaders who fall from grace, fall because

of one or more of the four 'G's - the *Girls*, the *Gold*, the *Glory*, the *Give up*. These represent sexual sin, abuse of money, abuse of power and the temptation to give up.

To me, the abuse of money and sexual sin are very obvious traps. People who fall into these traps are either stupid or lack commitment to their life purpose. Having been around several people who have fallen to one or other of these two temptations, I think it's easy to see them coming. People who commit adultery and then look surprised and say, 'It just happened', are completely deluding themselves. It never 'just happens'. It begins with wrong thoughts, followed by inappropriate moments, personal insecurity, a dissatisfaction with life and a growing sense of separation from their spouse. It is usually a result of not maintaining the relationship we have and a refusal to deal with problems. If you do not deal with your problems, your problems will deal with you.

The third temptation is the glory. I know people who are in love with being up front and on the platform. Standing at the front and having the attention of the crowd is a necessary part of being a public speaker. It is a great feeling to get applause or compliments after you have given a talk or ministered in some way. But to confuse your identity with that stage persona is very dangerous. I've read of celebrities who only live for the two hours they spend on a stage each night. The rest of their life is hell. If we do that, we're confusing our who with our do.

Standing on a stage or getting some sort of glory for doing something in public is what we *do*. But it is not *who* we are. People who live for fame are destined to fail at some point. The public image becomes too far removed from the reality to be sustained. Then the inner collapse comes.

Who we really are is who we are in the dark, who we really are when no one else is looking. We need to find peace with ourself in that situation. Living for public adulation will poison our private lives. It's the reason many musicians and singers start taking drugs when they have some success and get known in the media. Their charisma is bigger than their character. It is not sustainable.

Cults begin when people allow themselves to be put on a pedestal - or they put themselves on one. Then their followers are not allowed to ask awkward questions. The leader begins to live in a fantasy world where he or she can do no wrong. You see it in cults and in dictatorships. If you are standing on a pedestal, get off before it's too late.

The final temptation is to just give up. This

temptation comes when we are tired and the battle has been long. A feeling of futility sets in and we just want to quit. Now is not the time to quit. If we just press on a bit further we may get a breakthrough and make a difference to the world.

Charles Darrow brought the first prototype of the board game Monopoly to Parker Brothers in 1934. They laughed him out of the office. They said, "That's a really stupid game. Its never going to sell. Its far too complicated. It takes far too long to play. We are experts on games and we figure that there are 52 major flaws in this game of Monopoly."

But that did not deter Charles Darrow. He began to market the game on his own. Within one year one department store sold 5,000 sets.

It was such a success Parker Brothers confessed, "Maybe we were a little too hasty." They signed a contract with Charles Darrow and he became a multi millionaire. They have since sold 100 ,000,000 sets of Monopoly in 54 countries, in 26 languages, and 3.2 billion little green houses have been produced. If you took all these little green houses and put them side by side they would encircle the entire globe. Now is not the time to quit.

James Dyson noticed that most vacuum cleaners loose suction after cleaning only one room, because the pores in the bag clog with dust. It took him five years, hundred's of thousands of pounds of debts, and 5,127 prototypes to produce the worlds first bagless vacuum cleaner. He was constantly told "If there was a better way to design a vacuum cleaner, Hoover would have done it by now."

The Dyson DC01 vacuum cleaner is now the best selling vacuum cleaner in the world with sales of over £2 billion world-wide. James Dyson is now a multimillionaire. He had many opportunities to quit. He just didn't take any of them.

Anyone who has achieved anything in life has usually gone through times of trial and difficulty. Great things are not achieved by sitting on the sofa, eating donuts and watching trash TV. The Bible says,

> "Do not rejoice over me, my enemy; When I fall, I will arise; When I sit in darkness, The LORD will be a light to me." (Micah 7:8)

The secret to success in life is this: if you fall seven times make sure you get up eight times. There's nothing final about falling as long as you get back up. When I was learning to ride a bicycle I fell off many times. Sometimes there would be blood and tears. But I can ride a bicycle today because I kept getting back up and trying again. I'd seen others do it - I knew it was possible. I just needed to persevere. If you are tempted to give up right now, don't. Your breakthrough could be just around the corner. No one remembers the half-time score. It's the final score that counts. Giving up now will rob you of your destiny.

A prayer
Lord Jesus
Help me today to form a good character.
Speak to me about bad habits that are corrupting my character.
Give me wisdom and help me change my lifestyle and my habits.
This year, help me to establish things in my life that will form a character that is pleasing to you.
Help me to carry on when the going gets tough.
Be close to me today.
Amen

7. Detox your destiny

Esther was faced with a dilemma. The people of Israel were facing genocide. Esther knew she had some favour with the king and he might listen to her plea and save the Israelites. However, the law of the palace was that anyone entering the king's presence without being summoned was automatically put to death, unless the king said otherwise. Mordecai, her relative urged her to take a risk with her life in order to save the nation. And he suggested that this may actually be her destiny, her defining moment.

> "Who knows whether you have come to the kingdom for such a time as this?"
>
> (Esther 4:14)

There may come a moment in your life when you face a challenge and an opportunity to do great good. Maybe you were born for *such a time as this*. In any case, God has a plan for your life. It is a great plan and you need to get this plan clear from God.

> "For I know the thoughts that I think toward you, says the LORD, thoughts of peace and not of evil, to give you a future and a hope."
>
> (Jeremiah 29:11)

We need to get this plan from God. How do we find out what God's plan for us is? We ask him for wisdom and then we wait for revelation.

The Bible says, "If any of you lacks wisdom, let him ask of God, who gives to all liberally and without finding fault, and it will be given to him."

(James 1:5)

When I quote these words to God and then ask him to give me wisdom, I usually find that at some time that day or the next the wisdom or revelation I was looking for seems to come to my mind. I have learnt now, to ask God for wisdom on matters and then relax because he 'gives to all liberally and without finding fault'.

Once we have God's master plan for our life we need to *write it down*. We should be able to write it down in one sentence, or two or three short phrases.

For example, God's plan for my life is to '*Preach the gospel, Teach disciples, and Help the poor*'. Having your life purpose written down in a single sentence is very helpful. If I am asked whether I will do something by and individual or a church or group, I look and my purpose statement and ask, 'Is this task in any way - preaching the gospel, teaching disciples or helping the poor? If it isn't, I tend not to get involved.

Secondly, once we have our life purpose we

need to write down a plan of how we are going to bring it about. Some Christians say, 'Well, I'll just trust the Holy Spirit to lead me. I don't need a plan'. That is one of the most stupid statements I have ever heard. People like that don't know their Bible.

The Bible says, "Commit to the LORD whatever you do, and your plans will succeed."

"Make plans by seeking advice; if you wage war, obtain guidance."

"The plans of the diligent lead to profit as surely as haste leads to poverty."
(Proverbs 16:3, 20:18; 21:5, NIV)

If you fail to plan, you are planning to fail. So let me share with a little planning exercise I have used with many people. I really got a breakthrough with this plan. I used to draw it on scraps of paper when chatting to Bible students about their future. Since then I have taught it to groups using a powerpoint presentation. This plan gets results. I will lay it out here so you can fulfil your destiny. As I do so, you will see that we need to detox our life of obstacles that prevent us from walking in our destiny.

Your Destiny Action Plan
Step 1

Write your one sentence life purpose at the top of a sheet of paper like this:

My life purpose is to: ....

Step 2

Now write what you are currently doing or a short summary of your current life at the bottom of the sheet like this:

My life purpose is to: ....

My current life/work is:

Step 3

Now we can clearly see where we are and where we want to get to. Draw an arrow from bottom to top like this:

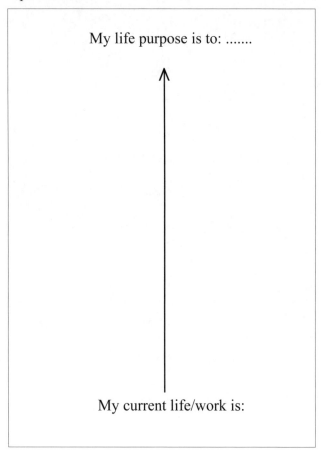

Step 4

List the obstacles which are preventing you from getting from the bottom of the paper to the top.

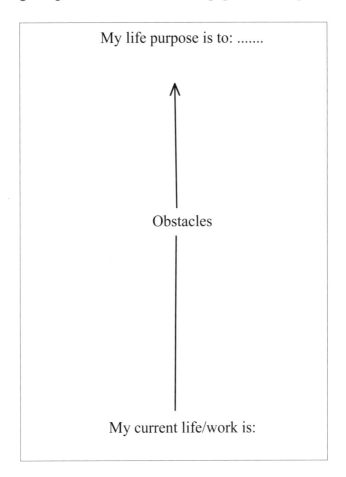

My life purpose is to: ....

Obstacles

My current life/work is:

Step 5
Now, for each obstacle, write down a possible solution. If there is more than one possible solution list them all.

Step 6
Now you need to put the solutions into a time scale. Create a **five year plan** for solving your obstacles. Make a list like this:

- Things I can do today
- This month
- Within three months
- Within six months
- Within one year
- Within three years
- Within five years

Please keep in mind that most people overestimate what they can achieve in one year but underestimate what they can achieve in five years.

Step 7
Carry out your plan. Making plans and then not acting on them is a complete waste of time. If you don't carry out your plan you are not really serious about reaching your destiny and you are

deluding yourself. Lots of people talk the talk but real achievers walk the walk. They walk out all the steps of their plan in reality.

Also remember that your plan is not set in concrete. If one strategy won't work explore other possibilities and ask God for more wisdom. Don't get stuck in a rut.

Don't neglect your character development. *How* you get there is as important as getting there. Short circuiting your destiny by using dubious means to reach it may destroy your destiny in the end.

A quick way to raise money for a project is to rob a bank. But robbing a bank will probably lead to your arrest and so your destiny is destroyed. Better to raise funds for a project through legal means. It will take a bit longer but you will avoid jail.

Let me repeat again, *how* you get there is as important as getting there. Some people leave a trail of people they have trampled over to reach their destiny. It's a stain on their character that will be with them for the rest of their life.

The detoxed lifestyle.

As you have worked through this book you will have seen that being cleansed in our mind and in our spirit can only be done in relationship with Jesus. He came to set us free. He came to set you free in your thoughts, words, actions, habits and character so that you can reach your destiny in Him. The Bible says, "If the Son makes you free, you shall be free indeed." (John 8:36)

Our soul, our real self is sometimes referred to as our heart. When we use the word 'heart' in this way, we are not referring to the lump of flesh that pumps blood round our bodies. We are referring to the centre of our being, that part of us that is made in God's image.

God said to the people of Israel, "I will give you a new heart and put a new spirit within you; I will take the heart of stone out of your flesh and give you a heart of flesh. I will put My Spirit within you and cause you to walk in My statutes, and you will keep My judgements and do them. Then you shall dwell in the land that I gave to your fathers; you shall be My people, and I will be your God."

(Ezekiel 36:26)

This word from God speaks of a relationship. Human beings became hard hearted towards God. Our heart was full of toxins that poisoned our relationship with our Creator. Now God offers us a new heart. He wants to remove the hard heart which he says is like a stone. He wants to give us a sensitive heart. He wants to put a new spirit in us so that we can have a real relationship with him. He wants us to 'walk' in his ways.

Maybe you didn't know you could have a relationship with God or maybe you're not sure if you have one or not. Jesus came to reconnect us with our Maker. The way to reconnect with God is to receive Jesus into our heart. The Bible says that Jesus came to his own people but his own people rejected him. Then it says that to all who do receive him, he gives power to become children of God. (John 1:12)

So we reconnect to God by receiving Jesus into our heart. How do we do that? In another place Jesus says it's like he's standing at the door to our heart and he is knocking on the door.

"If anyone hears My voice and opens the door, I will come in to him and eat with him, and he with Me."
(Revelation 3:20)

You see, it's about a relationship. Jesus wants to know you and he wants you to know him. As we follow Jesus we will walk in God's ways. Jesus said, "I am the way." As we walk in the way of Jesus our lives are transformed into his likeness. The purity of Jesus begins to affect us. A relationship with him will help us to detox our life continually. So how do we receive him?

He is standing at the door to your life today. You need to *invite* him to come in to your heart, into your life and welcome him. You need to put him first in all things.

A prayer of invitation
Lord Jesus
I want to walk in your ways.
I want to know your cleansing power today.
Please forgive me for the past,
for everything I did that was wrong.
Cleanse me from everything that has brought impurity into my spirit.
Wash me clean with your living water.
I now invite you into my heart, into the centre of my being.
Please come into my life Lord Jesus and set me free.
I open the door of my heart and give you control of my life.
I receive you now by faith.
Thank you Jesus.
Amen

You may or may not feel any different just now but if you said this prayer and meant it,

Jesus has come into your heart. It's not only about *feelings*, its about the *fact* that Jesus said he would come in. It's also about your *faith* - that you believe that Jesus has come into your heart.

As each day passes he will bring a new peace to your life - a peace beyond understanding. You have begun a new relationship with Jesus.

Talk to him. **Read** his words in the gospels every day. Meditate on his word and let him speak to you. Let his Holy Spirit come and dwell in you. His cleansing Holy Spirit will detox your very being.

As he reveals past hurts and other things you need to let go of or resolve, follow his leading and you will find true freedom and lasting peace.

May goodness and mercy follow you all the days of your life.

Become a life-changer today!

The RSVP Trust changes lives around the world. We currently change lives in the UK and Africa by:

- sponsoring the education of 300+ children
- meeting the costs of medical care
- feeding 100+ street children every week
- constructing and sponsoring the House of Mercy for 16 orphans
- reaching prisoners convicted of genocide
- restoring women involved in the sex trade
- giving educational scholarships
- helping people in Rwanda build a school for 700+ children
- visiting women involved in prostitution on UK streets
- feeding the starving through our Gifts of Hope scheme
- giving away hundreds of thousands of life changing books

and so much more!

Visit our website today and become a friend of the RSVP Trust.

www.rsvptrust.co.uk

By the same author:
- LIFE: what's that about?
- Overcoming the Storms of Life
- Grief Encounter - *finding hope when love ones die*
- A Word about your Healing
- The Rhythm of Life
- Stranger in the mirror